HENRY STEELE COMMAGER'S

AMERICANS

SOJOURNER TRUTH
and the Struggle for Freedom

BY EDWARD BEECHER CLAFLIN

Illustrations by Jada Rowland

CHILDRENS PRESS CHOICE

A Barron's title selected for educational distribution

ISBN 0-516-08588-3

To Jessie and Abigail

First edition published 1987
by Barron's Educational Series, Inc.

All inquiries should be addressed to:
Barron's Educational Series, Inc.
250 Wireless Blvd.
Hauppauge, NY 11788

Library of Congress Catalog Card No. 87-19325

International Standard Book No. 0-8120-3919-X

Library of Congress Cataloging-in-Publication Data
Claflin, Edward Beecher
  Sojourner Truth and the struggle for freedom.

  (Henry Steele Commager's Americans)
  Includes index.
  Summary: A biography of the black woman who was born a slave
and dedicated her life to the abolition of slavery and to improving the
living conditions of blacks following the Civil War.
    1. Truth, Sojourner, d. 1883—Juvenile literature.
2. Afro-Americans—Biography—Juvenile literature.
3. Abolitionists—United States—Biography—Juvenile
literature.   4. Social reformers—United States—
Biography—Juvenile literature.   [1. Truth, Sojourner,
d. 1883.   2. Afro-Americans—Biography.
3. Abolitionists.   4. Reformers]   I. Rowland, Jada, ill.
II. Title.   III. Series.
E185.97.T8C53   1987   305.5'67'0924   [92]   87-19325
ISBN 0-8120-3919-X

Printed in the United States of America
7 8 9   9693   9 8 7 6 5 4 3 2 1

CONTENTS

CONTENTS

When Harriet Beecher Stowe visited Abraham Lincoln in the White House, he asked her, "Is this the little woman who made the great war?" He might well have asked Sojourner Truth the same question when she visited him later that same year. Not many blacks received invitations to the White House in those years—or many women, for that matter, either. But this old black lady, who had given thirty years of her life to fighting slavery, was somebody very special.

Born a slave in New York, her only son had been torn from her arms and sold into slavery elsewhere. Although New York abolished slavery, the masters of Sojourner Truth refused to recognize the law. She managed to run away and, a few years later, to obtain her freedom from her former master. Then she tracked down the slaveowner who had taken her son to Alabama and won her son's freedom too. After that, there was no stopping her; she gave her life to the service of God, and to the freeing of the slaves.

Having a gift of simple and sincere eloquence, she swayed audiences wherever she spoke or sang. She never learned to write, but she dictated her story, the *Narrative of Sojourner Truth*, which sold widely in this country and in England. With limitless courage, she supported the cause of the "Underground Railway," that long chain of hiding places for slaves who had escaped across the Potomac or the Ohio Rivers into the North, Canada and freedom.

After the Civil War, she gave her energies, and her earnings, to settling ex-slaves in Kansas and Missouri, and to the vain attempt to persuade the Congress to set aside free land in the great West as farms for former slaves. Like the "forty acres and a mule" that Army officers had promised slaves who would join the Union ranks, nothing came of this. Championing the rights of women, as well as the rights of blacks, she was herself both saintly and courageous.

Henry Steele Commager
Amherst, Massachusetts

CHAPTER ONE

The Journey of a Sojourner

Sojourner Truth

HARDENBERGH ESTATE

By seven o'clock on January 1, 1871, a large crowd filled Tremont Hall in Boston. Though most of the people in the audience were white, they had come to celebrate a history-making event in black history. Just eight years before, Abraham Lincoln had signed the Emancipation Proclamation, declaring that ". . . all persons held as slaves . . . shall be free."

Those powerful words that had shaken a nation were still ringing in the ears of the crowd gathered in Tremont Hall. Among the group were many of the great "abolitionists," those who had worked in the cause to banish slavery from the United States of America.

Now, as the last ones found places in the pews and benches of the church, all eyes turned to the speakers' platform.

On the platform, alongside the church choir, were famous ministers, orators, and churchmen. There was even a medical doctor who was well known for his support of abolitionism. They were all elegantly dressed, wearing dark suits and high-collared shirts with black or white cravats (small, silk scarves knotted like bowties). Each came from a fine home. Most, if not all, had hired servants. They were well educated and wealthy, the cream of Boston's social elite.

The speeches began, led by the Reverend J. D. Fulton. As he finished, there was a sudden stir at the left side of the platform. The Reverend Fulton paused. All eyes turned to see who had arrived.

At that moment, onto the platform stepped a six-foot-tall, aged black woman. She had a strong-featured face, with a broad, gentle mouth and high cheekbones, framed by a close-fitting white cap that clung about her ears. A pair of wire-rimmed spectacles sat on her nose. But the eyes that peered from behind those spectacles had a piercing clarity that made the glasses seem unnecessary.

Her loose fitting gray dress swished about her ankle-high boots as she briskly crossed the platform.

Reverend Fulton stepped aside to offer his seat. "Now, Aunty," he said, "you take this easy chair."

Though he gave her the respect he might show toward an old woman, there were no signs of age as she nodded and took the seat. In her left hand was a large, leatherbound black book that she placed in her lap. With her right hand, she straightened the white, fringed shawl on her shoulders. As she did so, she kept the fingers of that hand tucked inward to hide an old injury.

A new sense of anticipation swept through the hall with the arrival of this black woman. A few whispers could be heard. All knew her by sight.

It was Sojourner Truth! This was the famous woman who had fought slavery and battled for constitutional equality and women's rights.

Her fame had traveled before her.

Even before slaves in the North were freed, Sojourner Truth had shown bold courage. In 1826, she walked away from her New York slave master.

When her son was sold to a cruel Southern plantation owner, she had brought the slave trader before a white man's court of law—and won her case!

For several years before the Civil War, she had traveled hundreds of miles alone. She carried only her few possessions—a smoking pipe, her carpetbag, and the "Book of Life," which she now held on her lap. Everywhere she traveled, she had preached freedom, equality, and a new life for every black American. Audiences had been swept away by her words. Controversy sprang up wherever she spoke.

This was the woman who carried food to the Union Army's only black regiment during the Civil War.

It was Sojourner Truth who took it upon herself to

travel to the nation's Capitol. Here, she shook hands with Abraham Lincoln and offered him her personal advice.

She was the first black woman to force her way onto an all white streetcar in Washington.

"Sojourner Truth." It was a name she had made up for herself. A Sojourner, or traveler, on earth. One who spoke the Truth. That was the creed she had made for herself—the way of life she followed.

Was it any wonder that the audience in Tremont Hall could hardly wait for the stately black woman to rise to her feet and begin speaking?

But even though everyone was eager to hear her speech, few were prepared for the message she delivered—or the way she spoke.

Her voice was as deep as a man's. As she peered out over the crowd, she could be heard in the farthest corners of the room.

She began simply, as she always did, addressing the group like a school class.

"Well, children," she said, "I'm glad to see so many together!"

But the words that followed sent shock waves through the audience.

"I only count my years from the time that I was emancipated. That's when I began. But God has fulfilled me, and the time that I lost being a slave has been made up. When I was a slave, I hated the white people. . . ."

With that, Sojourner Truth began to tell the story she had told many times before. It was the story of a child born in the cold, damp cellar of a slave owner in upstate

New York. It was the story of the long journey that brought that child to the present time.

There is no exact record of Sojourner's birth date, but it was probably about 1797. She was born about fourteen years after the end of the American Revolution. Her original name was not Sojourner. It was Isabella, and her mother and father called her Belle. The first home she ever knew was the grim, dark cellar of a stately limestone house on the plantation of Charles Hardenbergh.

The Hardenberghs, wealthy Dutch landowners, owned nearly two million acres between the Hudson and Delaware Rivers in Ulster County, New York. The house where Belle lived was in the town of Hurley, about eighty miles north of New York City.

Colonel Hardenbergh owned a dozen slaves. Men, women, and children all slept together in the same dark cellar. This is how one writer described that room:

> It was a dismal chamber, its only lights consisting of a few panes of glass, through which the sun never shown. The space between the loose boards of the floor and the uneven earth below, was often filled with mud and water. Inmates of both sexes and all ages slept on those damp boards, like horses, with a little straw and a blanket. Rheumatisms, fever-sores and palsies . . . racked the bodies of those fellow-slaves . . .

The first language that Belle learned was "low Dutch." This was the language first used by the Dutch

HARDENBERGH CELLAR

immigrants who settled in New York. It was the language spoken by her master. Both her parents had names that sound strange to us, because they were in that language. Her father was called "Baumfree," which is low Dutch for "tree," and her mother was called "Mau-Mau Bett."

Mau-Mau Bett and Baumfree had ten children. But by the time Belle was born, only she and her younger brother Peter remained at the Hardenbergh's plantation. All other brothers and sisters had been sold. Slave children were considered the master's property. Whenever the master had slaves he did not need, he took the youngest or weakest to auction.

Mau-Mau Bett remembered all of Belle's brothers and sisters by name. At night, sitting in the damp cellar lit by a blazing pine knot, she would tell stories about

6

the ones who had been taken away. With Belle and Peter at her knee, Mau-Mau Bett recalled the day when Belle's older brother and sister, Michael and Nancy, had been seized.

It had been a cold, snowy winter's day when Mau-Mau Bett lost Michael and Nancy. She recalled how Michael, who was just five years old, rose early to light the fire. As he knelt warming his hands by the blazing twigs, he suddenly looked up. From outside the house came the brisk jingle of sleigh bells.

He was very excited. The arrival of a winter sleigh with prancing horses was a real event! Michael rushed up the stairs from the cellar onto the snowy drive.

A prosperous looking white man in a big fur coat got out of the sleigh and went into the house. As soon as the man was gone, Michael hopped up in the sleigh, hoping he would be taken for a ride.

When the driver emerged a few minutes later, he was carrying Michael's three-year-old sister Nancy. To Michael's delight, the man in the fur coat carried Nancy directly to the sleigh.

So they were *both* going for a ride!

But Michael's anticipation soon turned to horror. The driver did not put Nancy on the seat of the sleigh. Instead, he opened the box in back that was for holding luggage. He shoved Nancy inside and slammed the lid down.

As Nancy began to scream and cry, the driver bolted the lid shut.

Then he turned toward Michael.

Only then did Michael realize what was happening. This was a slave trader. Nancy had been sold! In terror, Michael turned and raced toward the cellar to hide.

The white man was too quick. With a single sweep of his arm he caught up the little boy, lifted the lid of the sleigh box, and hurled Michael inside with his sister.

Mounting the seat of the sleigh, the man in the fur coat touched his whip to the horses. Jangling bells mingled with the screams of Mau-Mau Bett's children as the sleigh pulled out of the yard and glided down the road.

Listening wide eyed, Belle could imagine each moment of that dreadful day as Mau-Mau Bett told this story. The screams and pleas of her brother and sister rang in her ears as if she actually heard them. Even though she had never known Michael and Nancy, they were very much alive to her. Wherever they were now, they were still part of her family! Her mother loved those missing children so much that Sojourner could feel that ache in her own heart.

How could such a terrible thing happen?

Then a thought would occur to Belle that made her tremble and shake with fear. The same thing could happen to her!

She, Belle, belonged to Charles Hardenbergh. Mau-Mau Bett and Baumfree could not protect her. She was the possession of the man who lived upstairs in warm, well-furnished rooms with curtains at the windows. To him, Belle was just like his long-stemmed smoking pipe or his silk-embroidered armchair in his sitting room. He bought them and he could sell them—and her—anytime he wanted to.

Shuddering, Belle nestled closer to her mother and climbed into her arms. Mau-Mau Bett knew how Belle was feeling, but what could she say to comfort her child? She could not promise to protect her. That would be a false promise. She could not defy the white man. To do so would bring severe punishment—even death—to her or Belle.

There was only one way that Mau-Mau Bett could reassure her remaining son and daughter:

"My children," she said, "there is a God, who hears and sees you. He lives in the sky, and when you are beaten, or cruelly treated, or fall into any trouble, you must ask help of Him, and He will always hear and help you."

Was Belle comforted by these words? Perhaps.

But imagine what it would be like if your brother or sister could disappear anytime. You might never know what became of him or her. No one would tell you. Once separated, slave brothers and sisters could never count on seeing each other again.

Worst of all, each time the master called, it might signal your turn to be sold. It could happen anytime. This afternoon, tomorrow morning, in the middle of the night.

This possibility terrified Belle. Every time there was a call from the master upstairs, she looked at her mother and father with fear in her eyes. Would this be the moment that she was snatched away from them?

9

By the time she was nine years old, some of that fear had gone away. She was a skinny, active girl who worked hard. Nine years, and still she was living with her mother and father. Perhaps Master Charles Hardenbergh liked her well enough to keep her with Mau-Mau Bett and Baumfree forever.

Then, one day, one of the house slaves came down to the basement with dreadful news. Master Charles was sick!

They all knew what that meant. The death of a master would bring about change in the household. All of them might be sold!

Day after day the slaves waited for word that their master's condition had improved. But the house slaves who came down to the cellar always shook their heads. Master Charles was worse. His fever was rising. The doctors said there was nothing that could be done.

On the day Charles Hardenbergh died, the sounds of murmured prayers filled the cellar. The slaves prayed for his soul. But more, they prayed for God to look after them now. The master who had exercised a godlike power over them all these years was gone now. Who would take his place?

The day of the funeral, all the slaves watched solemnly as Master Charles's coffin was carried out to the black draped carriage. Some of them would miss Master Charles, because they considered him a kind master. He had not beaten them, as did many other slave owners.

But most of the slaves were thinking of what would

happen now. Belle looked up at her father. He was getting on in years, and he was thin and weak from the time spent in the cold, damp quarters under the house. What would the white people do with him when he could no longer work?

Belle's mother stood with bowed head. She was saying the Lord's Prayer for Master Charles. How much longer would Belle wake up to the comforting sound of her mother's voice repeating that familiar prayer?

When the carriage had pulled away, all the slaves talked among themselves. But Belle did not share in the gossip. She was lost in private fears. Terrible things were coming—she could feel it.

The days passed. Men came to look at the house. They called out the slaves and made them line up. A man in a gray frock coat pointed to Belle with his cane, a smirk on his face. He said something to the man standing next to him, and the two gentlemen laughed.

Belle lowered her eyes and folded her hands. She was afraid that if she looked directly at the white men they would see what she was feeling toward them at that moment. She hated them—their smirks and their comfortable laughter.

She knew what they were discussing. They were talking about selling her. And she knew why they were laughing. They thought she was worthless.

CHAPTER TWO

Sold!

Young Belle

SLAVE AUCTION

In the year 1806, Belle was put up for sale. A slave auction in New York was much like an auction in South Carolina, Georgia, or other parts of the South.

In a dusty yard under a shade tree, a platform was set up to display the slaves. Nearby, a few cows and horses grazed on the grass that sprouted from the dusty soil. A small pen held bleating sheep.

The slaves were gathered in an area where prospective buyers were free to examine them. They would look in a slave's mouth to see if the teeth were good, the same way they examined a horse's teeth. Landowners, merchants, and slave dealers squeezed Belle's muscles and examined her hands and feet to find out whether she was fit to work.

Her mother and father were not with her. The new owners of the Hardenbergh house had decided to free Baumfree. The old man was too weak to be useful any more. At that time, the law required a slave owner to pay a fee for setting free an old slave. So the new owners set free Mau-Mau, too, so that she could take care of Baumfree. This way, the owners wouldn't have to pay the fee.

But Belle was not free. She had to face the slave auction alone.

One by one, the slaves were led up onto the platform, while the auctioneer praised the strength and health of each one.

"One fine nigger wench," he bellowed when a black girl stepped up to the platform. "She's hale and young and straight, good for the field or house. Do I hear forty dollars? Who will give me forty dollars?" The bidding would continue fast and furious until the girl was sold.

Suddenly a hand clutched Belle's arm and she was yanked up onto the platform. She stood in front of all the staring faces, hands folded and eyes lowered. She jumped as the auctioneer bellowed her name.

"Hardenbergh's Belle!"

Belle hardly listened to the description that rattled off the auctioneer's nimble tongue. He was not talking about any Belle that she knew. He was describing market goods. All his words came down to one thing. He wanted a good price!

The auctioneer started her out at twenty dollars. Not

a single voice called out. The auctioneer lowered the price. "Ten dollars!" Still no bids. No one wanted her!

For a moment, Belle felt a ray of hope. Perhaps she would be returned to the Hardenberghs. If no one bid on her, she might go back to her mother and father!

The auctioneer whispered with one of the livestock owners. When he returned to the platform, he announced with a sweeping gesture that he was generously improving the offer. Along with the "nigger wench" he would sell one-half dozen sheep.

The bidding resumed at a brisk pace. Before Belle knew what had happened, she heard the roar of the auctioneer's voice as he called out, "Going once, going twice . . . SOLD!"

The smack of the gavel was like a gunshot.

With that, Hardenbergh's Belle and one-half dozen sheep were sold to John Neely, an English speaking dry goods merchant from Twaalfskill, New York.

What would you do if you suddenly moved in with people who spoke a language you had never heard before? If they told you to do something, you wouldn't know where to begin or even what they were talking about.

That was exactly Belle's situation with the Neelys. At the Hardenberghs, she had spoken only Low Dutch. Now she had to learn English—and she did not know a word.

When Mrs. Neely told Belle to fetch a frying pan, Belle had no idea what the mistress was demanding. A slave was not supposed to ask questions; she was expected to obey instantly.

So Belle tried to guess. Did Mrs. Neely want a pothook?

When Belle returned with a pothook, Mrs. Neely flew into a rage. Belle felt the woman's scorn, but she was trapped. How could she obey Mrs. Neely, when she could not understand a single word the woman was saying to her?

Mrs. Neely did not understand the girl's confusion. It seemed to her that Belle was just being obstinate and disobedient. There was only one way to cure Belle of that attitude. The girl had to be beaten into submission.

It was Mr. Neely who took Belle out to the barn. He tied together a bundle of rods and singed them in the fire. He bound Belle's hands and whipped her back until she bled.

She carried the scars for the rest of her life. Many years later she would say:

"When I hear them tell of whipping women on the bare flesh, it makes *my* flesh crawl, and my very hair rise on my head! Oh, my God, what a way is this of treating human beings?"

One snowy day, her father came to visit her at the Neelys. When Baumfree first came into the Neely house, Belle was afraid to say anything about how miserable she was. It was as if the walls had ears, and she feared Neely's punishment. But when Baumfree was ready to leave,

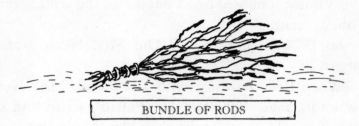

BUNDLE OF RODS

Belle followed him, stepping in the big footprints he left in the snow.

At the gate, beyond earshot of the Neelys, she told her father how she was beaten. She pleaded with him to find someone else who would buy her, so she would not have to spend the rest of her life with the Neelys. Baumfree said he would do what he could.

But even as he said the words to his daughter who stood trembling in the frozen snow, Baumfree must have known there was little that could be done. A slave had no influence over the white people who could buy and sell his children. At most, he could only tell the other slaves of her misery.

All during that bitter cold winter, the snow remained on the ground. Belle had no shoes or boots—only a few rags tied around her feet. After each of her father's visits, she walked out into the snow, stepping carefully in Baumfree's footsteps as she walked to the gate. From there she gazed across the snow-clad, rolling hills and prayed that someone would come to rescue her.

During the next few years, Belle was sold two more times.

The first buyer was a rough fisherman, Martin Schryver, who ran a tavern at the fork of the river between Kingston and Kingston landing. ,

Schryver treated her much better than the Neelys had. And Belle liked Kingston. Excitement seemed to hover around the tavern and ship landing. When Belle went down to the wharfside shops for a jug of molasses or liquor, she could watch the sailing ships and paddle wheelers come into the harbor.

By now, Belle had learned some English. She understood what people were saying in the tavern. When she brought pints of ale to the gruff men seated at the plank tables, she heard talk of far-off cities like Boston, New York, and Philadelphia. Her ears perked up as the men described exotic foreign countries—the West Indies, Africa, England, and France.

Belle was sharp witted, and she probably said a few things that made the men roar with laughter. The easygoing seamen were not as strict as the local Dutch and English landowners. What did they care if a saucy slave girl occasionally spoke her mind? They came to the tavern for amusement. Belle's quick tongue and tart observations were just part of the entertainment!

One day, a man who stopped at the tavern offered a sum for Belle that Mr. Schryver could not refuse. The price was almost three hundred dollars!

To the struggling tavern keeper, it was a fortune.

He could not refuse such a princely amount for a "nigger wench."

So "Schryver's Belle" became "Dumont's Belle," the property of John J. Dumont of New Paltz Landing. And once again, Belle found herself in a new home.

CHAPTER THREE

Dangerous Love

Catlin's Bob

BELLE'S HIDEAWAY

By the age of thirteen, when Belle moved into the Dumont household, she was tall and strong. At the Neelys and the Schryvers she had done many kinds of heavy chores. She had hoed corn, fetched wood, and toted five-gallon jugs and huge crates of fish.

Dumont soon found out how much Belle could do in a day. As he told one friend, "She is better to me than a *man*—for she will do a good family's washing in the night and be ready in the morning to go into the field, where she will do as much at raking and binding as my best hands."

Belle did not get extra rewards for her hard work. In fact, the two hired girls who worked for Mrs. Dumont conspired against her. One of them, Kate, pulled a particularly nasty trick.

It was Belle's responsibility to clean and boil the potatoes for the Dumonts' breakfast. Every day, she would get up early to stoke the fire, scrub the potatoes, and put water on to boil. Then she went out to do the milking while the potatoes were cooking over the fire.

In spite of Belle's care, each day the potatoes came out of the pot looking dirty. Mrs. Dumont flew into a rage. "This is a fine specimen of Belle's work!" she berated Mr. Dumont. "It is the way *all* her work is done!"

Dumont scolded Belle and told her to be more careful in the future.

What was wrong? Why did the potatoes always come out dirty? The Dumonts' ten-year-old daughter Gertrude had an idea. One night, Gertrude confided her suspicions to Belle. "I hate to see 'Poppee' and 'Matty' scold you so terribly," she said, calling her father and mother by the pet names she used. "And I know those dirty potatoes aren't your fault! I think Kate is doing it all!"

Belle looked at Gertrude in amazement. Here was a white girl—three years younger, and the master's daughter besides—taking her side! It was the first time any white person had ever stood up for her, and Belle felt a rush of gratitude.

As Belle continued to listen in wonderment, Gertrude proposed a secret plan. The next morning, Gertrude would remain in the kitchen and watch the potatoes when Belle went out to milk the cows. If Kate was playing tricks, Gertrude would soon find out!

The next morning, everything went according to plan. Belle scrubbed the potatoes thoroughly and put them on to boil. Then she went out to do the milking while Gertrude remained in the kitchen.

As soon as Belle was gone, the hired girl, Kate, came into the kitchen, carrying her broom. She seemed shocked to find Gertrude there, and she shooed Gertrude away to do some errand. When Gertrude refused to leave, Kate got very huffy, but she went about her work. She was just waiting for her chance. When she thought Gertrude was not watching, Kate suddenly lifted her broom from the hearth and dumped a huge black clump of ashes into the boiling water.

Shaking with anger, Gertrude slipped out of the room and rushed off to find her father. Wondering what all the disturbance was about, Mr. Dumont followed his daughter back into the kitchen.

"Poppee!" announced Gertrude, pointing at the hired girl, "Kate has been putting ashes in the potatoes. I saw her do it! Look for yourself. Belle washed them clean! It was Kate who made the potatoes so dingy every morning."

After that, Belle was never accused of sloppiness again.

As life at the Dumonts became easier, Belle began feeling more and more comfortable. The house was clean and well managed, and Mr. Dumont admired all the work that Belle could do. Mrs. Dumont was always snappish and difficult to please. But whenever Belle was feeling low, she reminded herself what Gertrude had done for her. That one act of kindness made a great difference in Belle's life at the Dumonts.

Belle felt at home among the house and field slaves. She shared many thoughts with them. They prayed and sang together. Soon, Belle had many friends she could talk to. Some of the older slaves treated her almost like their daughter.

The day came when Belle needed all the kindness she could find. A servant from the Hardenbergh estate came to the Dumonts to inform Belle that her mother, Mau-Mau Bett, was dead. She died of a stroke in the cellar where she had lived so many years.

Belle was given a rare day of freedom to attend her mother's funeral. There she saw Baumfree and Peter, who were still at the Hardenberghs'.

After that, meetings were rare. Masters begrudged their slaves any time off. And the distance from the Dumonts to the Hardenberghs was more than twelve miles. Even for a strong, tall girl like Belle, that was just too far for a day's walk.

During the early years at the Dumonts, Belle had little time to herself. Whenever she could escape notice, she slipped away. No one knew where she went, and Belle made sure that no one found out. She wanted some place that was all to herself.

Her secret hideaway was a small island in the middle of a nearby creek. The island was overgrown with willow trees and low bushes. Crossing the shallow creek and following a winding sheep path through the bushes, Belle came to a small clearing. There she made a shelter out of braided willow branches.

Years later, a friend described how Belle went to this private place to think and pray:

"Belle demanded . . . all her more pressing wants. . . . She felt as if God was under obligation to her, much more than she was to Him. He seemed bound to do her bidding."

There were many things Belle wanted. Why couldn't she have her own room and her own possessions? Why couldn't she come and go as she pleased? Why did she always have to answer, "Yes, master" and "Yes, ma'am," every time the Dumonts wanted something of her?

Secluded in her island, under the willow boughs, she was free to dream. She could imagine setting out on a long road that led to places she had never been before. She could think about boarding one of those tall sloops that she had seen in the river.

Some of her thoughts were sad. Safe in her private place, she thought of the cruelty that her mother, her father, and all her family had endured—and she thought about the scars of whippings on her own back.

More and more often, Belle tried to slip away to her island. Soon she was visiting it almost every day.

But as time passed, she began thinking less about her own troubles, and asking less from God. Instead, she was beginning to think about a slave of her own age who belonged to the neighbor Catlin. His name was Robert, but everyone called him "Catlin's Bob."

Catlin's Bob was the most handsome young man that Belle had ever seen.

Slave owners disapproved of romance between slaves. Particularly forbidden was any love between slaves who belonged to different owners. What if the two slaves wanted to marry? Which household would they belong to? Who would own them? Who would own their children?

Both "Dumont's Belle" and "Catlin's Bob" knew the danger of being seen together. If their owners heard about their meetings, they might be whipped. Belle was not so fearful for herself, because mostly Dumont treated her well. But everybody knew that Bob's owner, Catlin, was extremely cruel.

Still, she couldn't help seeing Bob.

Every year, there was one holiday when the slaves from every household were allowed to mingle together. Seven weeks after Easter, the Dutch of Ulster County celebrated a seven day vacation called Pinkster.

For field and household slaves, Pinkster was a time of freedom. All slaves were released from work or they were paid like free workers. During Pinkster week they could do pretty much what they pleased.

In Ulster County it was the custom for the slaves to gather near a great oak tree. A tall, powerfully built slave dubbed "Prince Gerald" was dressed up in a fancy costume. Above his bare legs, he wore an old Revolutionary

PRINCE GERALD

War jacket with colored ribbons hanging from brass buttons. On his head was a little black hat with a pompom. His throne was a hollow log.

For seven days and nights there was steady singing and drumming as all the slaves danced together. Only occasionally, they would pause to sleep! When they woke up, they feasted on summer sausage, gingerbread, and last October's cider. Resting, eating, dancing, then resting again, they continued the happy round until they could dance no more.

Caught up in the swirling celebration that continued day and night, Belle felt more free and joyful than ever before. For seven days of glorious freedom, she did not have to say "Yes, master" or "Yes, ma'am" to anyone.

She was consumed with the music and dancing. She was thrilled whenever Robert touched her hand. And she thought she could never be happier, in her whole life, than she was on the night when he first kissed her!

After the Pinkster holiday was over, it was more difficult to see Robert. There were times when each of them could slip away. They would meet at night, hold each other tightly, and talk in low, secretive voices about the dreams they shared. Belle was certain that somehow they would find a place where they were free to love. Then they would be married!

But they must have known it was impossible. They must have been terribly afraid. Perhaps it was fear itself that made them more reckless than they should have been.

One Saturday afternoon when Belle was ill, she was surprised to see Mr. Dumont come into her sleeping quarters. He asked whether she had seen Catlin's Bob that day.

Belle tried to hide her alarm. Dumont had never mentioned Catlin's Bob in her presence before.

"No," she said simply, "I have not seen him."

"If you do," Dumont continued, "tell him to take care of himself, for the Catlins are after him."

All afternoon, Belle watched from the window,

praying that Bob would not try to come see her. But someone had told Bob that Belle was sick, and he would not stay away.

As Belle was looking out, her eyes caught a distant figure coming! It was Robert crossing the fence that bordered the Dumont and Catlin property.

At that moment, two white men rushed up behind him brandishing sticks. They were Master Catlin and his son! Her heart pounding, Belle threw open the window to shout a warning to Robert.

Too late!

With flailing sticks, the Catlins dragged Robert to the ground. Belle felt a sickness rise in her throat. The Catlins battered Robert without mercy. Their sticks rose and fell, and rose and fell, again and again. Abruptly, a loud, commanding voice interrupted them. Mr. Dumont rushed toward them.

"Off my property with your slave," he ordered. "I will not have human blood spilled on my premises."

Dragging Robert to his feet, the Catlins tied his hands with a rope and led him away. Dumont followed close behind.

A while later, Belle heard a footstep outside her door. Mr. Dumont came into the room and looked down at her. Belle was still trembling. Her cheeks were wet with tears.

"Their wrath has cooled," Mr. Dumont said gently. "I do not think they will strike him any more."

But Belle could hear the uncertainty in his voice.

During the endless weeks that followed, Belle prayed that Robert would not try to visit her again. She knew that if he was caught a second time, there would be little hope for him. .

More than anything on earth, she wanted to see him, hold him, and dress his wounds. But trying to see him would only risk terrible punishment, far worse than he had already known.

She blamed herself almost as much as the slave owners for what had happened. The greatest favor she could do for Robert now was to stay away from him. She should never try to see him again.

She tried to erase from sight all she had seen in the Dumont yard that day. Yet she could not forget her last glimpse of Robert as he fell to his knees, bloody and broken.

And his only crime was loving her.

Weeks went by before a slave finally came from the Catlin house with news of Robert. The inevitable had finally happened. Catlin had forced Robert to marry a slave in the Catlin household.

Belle could not explain her feelings. She should have felt better, knowing that Robert was still alive. Why didn't she feel relieved? Now that he was married, perhaps he would be happy without her.

But knowing that Robert was forced to marry someone else was painful to Belle. What had become of their love? How terrible that it could just be crushed, forgotten, and swept aside that way!

The blow was almost more than Belle could bear.

Now, when she visited her island retreat, she did not know whether to make demands on God, to beg Him for escape from the world, or to curse Him.

But there was little time to spend by herself. Ever since her illness, Belle had been working harder than ever for the Dumonts. But all her work was still not enough. There was still one more thing she must do for them.

She had to bear children.

Mr. Dumont had decided on her husband. Belle was to marry an older field hand who had been married twice before. His name was Thomas—more often known as "Dumont's Tom."

CHAPTER FOUR

First Steps to Freedom

Belle's Children

ROAD TO FREEDOM

Belle married Thomas in 1814. They lived together for about ten years. During that time she had five children, four of whom lived through infancy—Diana, Peter, Elizabeth, and Sophia.

Belle never stopped working. Soon after a child was born, she would put the baby in a basket, carry the basket out to the fields, and suspend it between two trees. A slave child would gently swing the basket until the baby woke up and began to cry. At the sound of the infant's voice, Belle stopped hoeing and came across the field to nurse the child.

30

In 1817, three years after her marriage, Belle heard news that thrilled her. The New York state legislature had passed a law that decreed all New York slaves born before July 4, 1799 would be freed on July 4, 1827. In 1799, a law had been passed that stated all slaves born from 1799 on would be free after they became twenty-five years old. Because Belle had been born in 1797, that law did not include her! Now this new law gave her freedom, too!

Ten years was a long time—but compared to a lifetime of slavery, the time seemed brief. A new promise was on the horizon; a hope would now be a reality. Belle could look forward to *freedom*!

Patiently she waited . . . and worked. Early in 1824; three years before Belle was lawfully entitled to be released, Mr. Dumont made her a promise. He said if she continued to work hard for him, he would hand over her and Tom's freedom papers on July 4, 1826, a whole year ahead of schedule.

Belle was elated. That meant one year less of slavery!

Then, a few months after Mr. Dumont's promise, Belle had an accident. Working in the fields, she cut her hand with the curved, razor-sharp blade of a scythe. The injured hand took a long time to heal because she continued to work, trying to do everything Mr. Dumont demanded of her.

She counted the days to freedom. The months passed. At last came July 4, 1826. The long awaited moment had arrived!

All day, Belle waited for the precious words that

would spell her liberation from bondage. Every time Dumont approached her, she expected him to say, "Belle, I promised you freedom, and this is the day. You are a free woman!" Any moment, she expected him to hand her the papers that declared her legally free from servitude. But the sun set with no words spoken between them.

Another day passed, then another. Had he forgotten? What was wrong?

Finally, Belle decided to remind Mr. Dumont. It was a bold thing for a slave to do. In fact, it was dangerous. No one questioned the master. Most slaves would not dare to remind a white man of any promise at all, much less a promise that he had made many years before.

But Belle dared! And the answer she received shattered what little faith she had in a master's word.

Dumont reminded her that she had injured her hand. Therefore, he said, he had lost nearly a year of work from her. He expected her to remain with him until she had made up the lost time. For sixteen years she had served Master Dumont. Yet he was punishing her for what he said was one year of "lost time."

Later, she realized that many slaves went through similar experiences with their masters:

"Just think of us! *So* eager for our pleasures, and just foolish enough to keep feeding and feeding ourselves up with the idea that we should get what had been thus fairly promised. And when we think it is almost in our hands, we find ourselves flatly denied!"

But Belle could not be denied any longer. She set

herself a single task to accomplish before she left—to spin a hundred pounds of wool that had been set aside for her. With the completion of that service, she decided, her obligation to the master would come to an end.

Just at sundown on a clear autumn day, Belle finished spinning the last of Dumont's wool.

Later the same night, she gathered all her small possessions in a cotton pillowcase. Quietly, she went to see her sleeping children. They were old enough to fare well without her, and she knew they would be safe and fairly treated by Dumont.

Then she picked up her youngest baby, Sophia, who was still at the nursing age. Moving silently among the sleeping slaves, Belle left the quarters and started down the long carriageway that led away from the Dumont house.

Once beyond sight of the house, she moved quickly, trying to put distance behind her. How far could she go in one night? She was traveling on foot and carrying a child! Dumont would certainly find her if he tried. He might try to force her to return. What would she do then?

Her pace quickened. The night surrounded her with familiar sounds, but the road was new to her. Dark shadows lurked on every side. The child in her arms seemed to grow heavier with each step.

What should she do? Where could she go? With each step, those questions turned in her mind.

By the time the pink dawn broke over the rolling hills, Belle was exhausted. She stopped for a moment. As

Sophia slept soundly and warmly in her arms, Belle gazed at the rising sun.

Suddenly the realization swept over her: "I am free!"

Daylight meant danger. She could be seized, dragged back to the Dumonts, and beaten for disobeying. But even that would not change what she was tasting now for the first time. Freedom!

No matter what Mr. Dumont said or did, she would never be a slave. Belle had escaped her master—*all* masters—forever.

Perhaps Belle would not have been so sure of herself if she could have looked into the future and seen the many hardships that lay ahead.

In 1827, slaves who were freed by law had few opportunities. Though slave owners were forced to free their slaves, they did not have to give their servants anything else—no money, jobs, or homes. Turned out by their masters, the former slaves found themselves wandering through the lush Catskill farmlands, poverty stricken and homeless. Some years before, Belle's father had been set free, only to discover the emptiness of freedom for an old man who is homeless, jobless, and without family. Baumfree had gone to live in a shack. When he fell sick, there was no one to care for him. He died alone.

The day after Belle left Dumont, she was just like one of those newly freed slaves. She was a strange, lone figure walking down a dusty road, carrying a baby on one arm, and holding a pillowcase in her crippled hand. She had no money, no home, and no destination. She had traveled all night, and she was exhausted and hungry. She had no idea where her next meal would come from.

Yet something inside her felt different. She had taken a bold stand. She had dared to defy her master. But how could she turn that newfound feeling of freedom into milk and bread for her child, and a place to rest her head at night?

In years to come, she would find herself in this fix again and again—striking out alone on a journey without knowing where she would end up. Each trip started out with hope and blind faith, and many ended in vain. But the promise she made to herself was always kept—to see the journey to the end, no matter what happened.

As Belle kept walking that day, she realized that she was near the home of a man she knew, Levi Rowe. She found her way to his door. Rowe had offered to help her years ago. He still wanted to help; but he was sick and bedridden. He told her to go on to see Isaac and Maria Van Wagenen, a Quaker couple who lived just down the road.

Belle thanked Mr. Rowe for his assistance. Wearily, she lifted Sophia onto her arm, and set out again along the dusty road. The sun was high now, and many carriages and wagons passed her by. Their drivers scarcely gave her a glance. With so many blacks being freed, a former slave walking along the side of the road was beginning to be a common sight.

After many miles Belle came to a neat clapboard house set back from the road behind a hedgerow. A plump woman in a dark dress was weeding the garden. As Belle turned into the yard, the woman got to her feet.

"Welcome," the woman said without a moment's hesitation. "What brings thee here?"

In a rush, Belle explained how she had gone to Levi Rowe for help, and he had sent her here. When she was finished, she waited for the woman's reply. What if she was sent away?

To Belle's relief the woman held out her hands to take the baby.

"Come inside," she smiled. "We have had our meal, but there is fresh corn bread for thee and milk for the baby."

While Belle was eating and feeding the baby, Mr. Van Wagenen came in from the field. Belle told the Van Wagenens about her life, and about how Mr. Dumont had lied to her. The Van Wagenens offered her work and a place to sleep. Belle accepted gratefully. But she feared that Dumont would soon catch up with her. Undoubtedly he was already asking questions in town to find out if anyone had seen a tall black woman with a baby, walking along the road.

Sure enough, Dumont appeared at the Van Wagenens a few hours later.

"Where is she?" Dumont demanded.

"Welcome to my house," said Mr. Van Wagenen calmly. "What is it you want?"

"That's my slave!" Dumont declared, pointing at Belle. "She comes back with me now!"

"It is no man's right to own another human being," said Mr. Van Wagenen. He thought a moment. "If you take her back, you must soon free her by law. In a few months, she will no longer be yours. I will pay you twenty dollars now if you leave her in peace. And I will pay five dollars for the child. I am not buying your slaves. I want no slaves. I only want their freedom."

Under the firm gaze of Mr. Van Wagenen, Dumont's rage cooled. The offer made good business sense. Better to have money in the pocket than a rebellious slave who would run away again.

Dumont accepted the offer.

As she watched him leave the house and climb into his carriage, Belle felt an overwhelming sense of relief. She hugged Sophia tightly to her. She and her child were free at last!

The Van Wagenens were Quakers, quiet, gentle people who never sang or raised their voices. They dressed in gray or black clothes, and went to Sunday Meeting where the congregation sat in silence throughout the service.

Like most Quakers, they believed that all slaves should be free. Although the landholders who lived around them had owned slaves for decades, the Quakers never did.

Belle was glad she had found people who accepted her as an equal. She cared greatly for her little daughter

Sophia. But she missed her other children and the slaves who had been her friends at the Dumonts. There were times when she was so lonely, she wanted to get away from the quiet, drab Van Wagenen house and return to the Dumont farm.

Then she heard what had become of her son Peter. All thoughts of returning to Dumont vanished forever.

Some time before, Dumont had sold Belle's five-year-old son, Peter, to a friend, Dr. Gedney. Belle had been told that Dr. Gedney would take the boy to England as his personal servant. But instead, Dr. Gedney handed Peter over to his brother, Solomon Gedney. Then Solomon sold Peter to his brother-in-law, a rich Alabama farmer named Fowler. If Peter was in the South, it meant he would never be free!

At that time, New York State laws specifically stated that owners could not sell slaves in other states. When Belle heard what had happened, she set out to confront those who had broken the law. Leaving Sophia in the care of the Van Wagenens, Belle headed for the Courthouse in New Paltz. She was determined to bring Solomon Gedney into court to face charges against him. She would *demand* the return of her son!

It was unheard of for a black woman—just recently a slave—to sue a white man. Soon the buzz of gossip went through New Paltz. This woman had been spending too much time with the Quakers, they said. She was getting foolish ideas into her head.

Everyone thought that she would be turned down by the judge, and then quietly go away. But they underestimated Belle.

First she confronted Mrs. Dumont face-to-face with Mr. Dumont's lie. Then she found a judge in the New Paltz Grand Jury courtroom and demanded that Solomon Gedney be brought to trial. She pursued the constable to make sure the summons was delivered to the correct person. Then she hired a lawyer, soliciting money from many Quaker friends so she could sue for her son's release.

In autumn of 1827, just when everything was ready for trial, Solomon Gedney left the state taking Peter with him.

Belle had to wait still longer.

But Solomon Gedney returned to New Paltz the following spring. Gedney must have thought he could keep his visit a secret. But again he had underestimated Belle. She was the first to find out that Fowler had brought her son back to town. She hired another lawyer who succeeded in bringing Solomon Gedney to the courtroom. And Peter was with him!

At last, Belle saw her son—and, for the first time, she came face to face with Solomon Gedney.

But Peter's first reaction to the sight of his mother was strange.

He turned away from her in the courtroom. Every now and then he glanced up at Mr. Gedney, as if imploring his approval. When the judge asked Peter whether he wanted to return to his mother, Peter fell to his knees. He said he had never seen this old woman before. He begged the judge not to take him away from Solomon Gedney who had done so much for him.

Fortunately, the judge was alert. He saw a ragged scar on Peter's forehead and another on his cheek. The judge also noticed that when Peter talked, he kept his fearful eyes on the slave trader. Peter could not muster the courage to look at his own mother!

Clearly, the boy feared punishment from the slave trader standing by him in the courtroom. With a single glance, it seemed, Solomon Gedney could decide his fate!

The judge ruled in favor of Belle. Her argument won. Gedney had broken the law. He had transported a slave to another state. Peter was her son. By law, he must be returned to her.

When Gedney finally left the courtroom, the justice, the attorney, and Belle all reassured Peter. He did not have to be afraid any more. Gedney was gone forever. Peter was free to live with his mother—not with that evil man!

Some days later, Peter told his mother everything that Mr. Fowler had done to him. He showed her the scars all over his body.

Many years after, when Belle told audiences what her son had suffered, people would fall silent out of respect for the ordeal that Peter had endured.

Mr. Fowler was not a human being. No human could treat a five-year-old boy as Peter had been treated.

Mr. Fowler was a monster. A monster in human costume, perhaps, but still a monster.

CHAPTER FIVE

City of Promise

Belle and Peter

SOUTH STREET NEW YORK

S oon after Peter rejoined his mother, they moved
into the town of Kingston, where Belle joined
the Methodist church. At first, Peter shied away
from people, as if they were going to beat him.
But gradually he became more lively, and as the days
went by, he turned into a happy little boy!

His mother made sure of that. Now Peter had other
boys to play with. Soon he was joining in their games—
racing through the woods playing "bear-hunt," hugging
the neighbor's cat, climbing up the haymow in the stable
loft. Best of all, he liked to dash across the wharves alongside the riverfront. When the ships came in, he would
hang around listening to the sailors' stories.

Seeing her son happy brought joy to Belle. She saved
the few coins she got from housework to buy Peter a

secondhand dark suit. Proudly he went with her to church every Sunday. All during the service he sat restlessly in the pew, swinging his legs. When the last "amen" had sounded, he slipped down the aisle ahead of his mother, escaping into the bright sunlight.

The active boy caught the attention of a schoolteacher, Miss Gear, who had come up from New York City to visit friends in Kingston. She was impressed by the proud bearing of the boy's mother. After church one morning, the schoolteacher came to Belle and began talking to her about her son.

Was Peter in school? she wondered. And what were Belle's plans for the boy?

Belle was overjoyed that someone took an interest in Peter—his boundless energy, his curiosity, his affection. How could she give him *real* freedom, the freedom to learn?

Miss Gear had an idea. Why didn't Belle and Peter come to New York City with her? She knew a good school that would accept him, and she herself would take care of the cost.

To listen to her, there was no other city like it! Everywhere you looked there were fashionable houses. The rich were always looking for servants. It would be easy to find a place for Belle—and maybe for Peter too.

Belle knew that Peter should have this opportunity. And once her mind was made up, nothing could stand in her way. Through her own determination, Belle had won her freedom. She had faced down slave dealers in a white man's court and won justice for her son. Now her son was growing up, getting smarter and stronger every day. He needed opportunities that he would not find in the stables and along the wharves of rural Kingston.

But Belle hesitated. There was her baby daughter Sophia to consider.

If Peter went to New York, Belle knew she would have to go with him. But she could not bring Sophia along. The child was too young. Belle would not be able to keep a job if she had to care for a toddler in the busy city.

There was only one solution. Belle would have to leave Sophia behind. Diana and Elizabeth would have to take care of her at the Dumont farm.

Belle felt sad about leaving her youngest child behind. But she knew that Diana and Elizabeth would be good to their younger sister.

The next time Miss Gear talked about New York City, Belle was ready with her answer. Yes, she and Peter were ready to go!

That very month, they were on their way. Peter's eyes were wide as he mounted the gangplank on to the great, white-sailed sloop. Although he had spent many hours along the wharves, he had never once been aboard one of these river ships. Now, he and his mother were sailing away, sailing to New York City!

Miss Gear was true to her promise. Seeing that Peter was interested in ships, she enrolled him in a navigation school. He would learn how to handle ships and find a course by the stars! Miss Gear raised the money to pay for his expenses. She also helped Belle find housework with a Mrs. Garfield on Nassau Street. Belle paid for her room and board by doing the household chores.

In 1829, New York City was not at all like it is today. All the big homes were at the tip of the island, especially around the docks and wharves.

New York was small, but it was already densely crowded and hard to get around in. Pigs roamed the broad cobblestone streets, rooting around in piles of rotting vegetables in front of stalls. Wharves were crowded with bales and boxes. Crossing any street was hazardous. In those days, people had to watch out for rattling carriages, clanging streetcars, fidgety horses, rumbling carts drawn by stubborn kicking mules, and handcarts pushed by gruff, burly dock workers.

The city also had its hidden corners of crime and its slums. If you asked the right person at the wharves, you could find out where slaves could be found. Although buying and selling slaves was forbidden, an underground trade in them still flourished.

If you wanted to find out how the poor lived, you would be taken to a dingy, smelly building called the Five Points, near the Bowery. Conditions were so horrible there that people said you could hear groans and howls coming from the tenements all night long. Many were afraid to go near at night, for fear of being murdered.

In a city as unfamiliar and strange as this, Belle searched for a church that she could attend. From the Methodist congregation in Kingston she had a letter of introduction to a Methodist church on New York's John Street. After a polite interview with one of the deacons, she was told that she was welcome to attend, but she would have to go to a separate service for "colored only."

Clearly, blacks were not encouraged to worship with whites in the Methodist church! Politely and firmly, though she was secretly seething with anger, Belle withdrew her request for membership.

Instead, she joined the Zion church on Church Street. It was an all black church. But the important thing to Belle was that she could attend any service she pleased! She had not come this far only to be told when she was allowed to worship and in whose company.

Many religious leaders had been drawn to Manhattan and Brooklyn where they could always attract a following. There were enough people in that crowded city to fill hundreds of churches. Once they had their audience, leaders spoke out harshly against the crimes, evils, and the temptations of corruption, all of which could be seen in every tavern, tenement, and alley.

Before long, Belle was drawn to one of the most magnetic religious leaders in New York, Elijah Pierson. Pierson thought it was his mission not only to cast out evil but also to draw followers into his self-styled "Kingdom of God." He formed a group of intensely devoted believers who contributed their money to a central bank account that belonged to the "Kingdom."

Belle became one of those followers. She went to work for the Piersons and gave everything she had earned to the kingdom. Like many of Pierson's converts, she was led to believe that another man, who called himself "Matthias," was the new Messiah. Belle hoped that Pierson and Matthias were everything that they appeared to be. She desperately wanted to help them build a new and better world than the one she had known.

Soon Belle realized what a terrible mistake she made by joining the "Kingdom" and giving up her freedom of choice. Her faith in those men received a powerful jolt when she realized they had squandered all the money she gave to them. Everything Belle had saved was gone!

A worse shock was to follow. One day when Belle was in Pierson's house, he suddenly became delirious, then paralyzed. A doctor rushed to save him, but there was no hope. Within hours, Elijah Pierson was dead. The doctor said he had been poisoned.

Belle was accused of poisoning him! Her name appeared in the newspaper, again and again. A muckraking reporter cast suspicion over everything she had done with the "Kingdom of God" group. Luckily the editor of an independent newspaper took up her cause and proved, logically and factually, that she could not possibly be suspected.

Her name was finally cleared.

Something good came from Belle's bad experience with the followers of the "Kingdom of God." For the first time in her life, Belle spoke in front of a white audience.

It was a turning point for her because it was the first time she realized the power of speech at her command.

Belle's first public speaking was probably at a meeting held by James Latourette, one of Pierson's followers, near Five Points. Five Points was in one of the poorest, filthiest areas of New York. Belle thought the poor folk in Five Points were worse off than any slave in Ulster County. A crowd had gathered from the streets to listen to John Maffitt, a well-known Irish-born Wesleyan preacher. With the encouragement of Mr. Latourette, Belle began speaking to a second group nearby.

She began in a low voice, but the novelty of a black woman addressing an audience soon drew people to her. As she gathered confidence, her voice rose. Her piercing dark eyes riveted the attention of her listeners. They were spellbound by her gaze and her message.

Someone handed her a Bible. She took it in her hands but did not open it. She could not read. Besides, she did not need the help of a book! She knew all the biblical passages by heart.

As more and more people drifted away from the famous John Maffitt toward the unknown woman with the deep, sure voice, Belle felt a new sense of power. They were listening! They wanted the word of God—but much more than God's word was on her lips. She had a story to tell, her own story.

She herself had escaped from one kind of slavery. But slavery took many forms. Oppression could be seen everywhere. She would open people's eyes. She would help them understand. She would free them!

Her voice gathered fervor as the crowd listened, spellbound, to what she had to say. They were all changed a little bit by the voice of the black woman who spoke to them that day.

The greatest change was in Belle herself. That day, she realized that a part of herself had been locked away. Now it had been released! She would never remain silent again.

Whereas Belle was gathering a stronger sense of faith and conviction, the city was having an opposite influence on her son Peter.

One day, a friend of Belle's told her that she had seen Peter in the street with a group of rowdy boys. He was supposed to be in school!

Belle questioned Peter, but his answers were evasive. Finally, she inquired at the navigation school he was supposed to be attending. She found out he never went to classes. He had taken the money meant for his education and spent it somewhere else.

But where? What had he done with it?

When Belle tried to question him, she almost went wild with frustration. Peter was lying to her! But he seemed indifferent. Whether he was telling the truth or lying, it all seemed the same to him. All he cared about was getting away from her accusing questions so he could join his friends on the street.

What did the street boys do all day? What were they up to?

If Peter could tell her that, Belle might have made sense of it all. But he couldn't—or wouldn't. Threats of discipline had no affect on him. Surely any kind of punishment would be a joke after what he had endured, as a five-year-old boy, at the hands of the murderous Mr. Fowler.

Peter was proud, stubborn, and independent. Now he knew his way around the streets. He did not have time for his mother's lectures and preaching. Her high expectations and great principles were not his concern.

Peter wanted to enjoy himself!

It was impossible to talk sense into him. But Belle persisted in trying. She found him a situation as a livery hand. The job was a good one, and easy enough. All Peter had to do was tend horses, rake stalls, and clean the harnesses, bridles, and saddles.

For a time, everything seemed to go well. Then one day, Belle received word that Peter was locked up in New York's dreaded jailhouse, the Tombs. The reason? He had stolen a harness from the stable and sold it on the street!

Belle was frantic with worry. She had fought so hard to win Peter's freedom—and this was how he chose to repay her! What could she do with him now?

Worst of all was the shame. Belle had to meet with Peter's employer and plead with the man not to press charges against her son. If the stable master would give Peter a break, Belle assured him, she would make sure such a thing never happened again. Her son was not going to become a criminal!

As it turned out, very little pleading was necessary. The stable master insisted on being repaid for the harness. Of course he would not rehire Peter, but, on the other hand, he did not intend to press charges. No one wanted

PETER IN THE STABLE

to keep the boy locked up in that grim jailhouse. As everyone knew, the Tombs was just a place where criminals learned more crime from hardened thiefs, murderers, and con artists.

Again, Belle won her son's freedom.

Again, Peter promised his mother that he would never break the law.

But to himself he was thinking that he would never be *caught* breaking the law. Out on the streets again, he soon fell in with the same crowd. Once more he was arrested. And once more, Belle arranged his release.

When Peter was thrown in the Tombs for the third time on a charge of thieving, Belle refused to come see him. Her patience had come to an end. She could no longer accept responsibility for the behavior of a son she could not control.

Peter was making his own choices now. He knew

the consequences of his choices. When a messenger from the prison told Belle that Peter had asked for her, she just shook her head. She did not know which was greater, her sadness that she no longer understood her son, or the anger that he threw away the opportunities that she won for him.

Belle could not blame Peter alone. She still felt hatred for the man who had beaten her unprotected, five-year-old Peter until the child's back was sticky with blood. That slavemaster could not be blamed for what Peter was doing now. But Belle knew that the deepest scars inflicted by the evil man had never healed.

CHAPTER SIX

A New Mission

La Tourette Meetings

PADDLE WHEELER

Belle did not turn her back on Peter. She simply left the choice in his hands. He was no longer a little boy playing pranks, and she could not keep bailing him out of jail. If he wanted to change his life, he would have to take the first step for himself.

And that was precisely what Peter did.

Among his street friends, he had taken on the name "Peter Williams," which also happened to be the name of a very kind black barber who lived in the city. Sitting on a cast-iron cot in a lonely jail cell, gazing out through the bars, Peter tried to think of some way out of jail. It occurred to him: why not get in touch with the barber of the same name?

Peter did not really believe the man would help him, but he had nothing to lose by trying!

As it turned out, it was the best thing he could have done. Peter Williams, the barber, *was* interested in the plight of this boy with the same name. He went to visit Peter in the Tombs. Something about the young Peter's stubborn determination caught the barber's interest. He saw evidence of many good qualities that had been twisted by street life: pride that had turned to swaggering, intelligence turned to shrewdness, and a sense of self-worth that had been transformed into self-righteousness.

The good qualities were still there, plus there was something else about the boy. Peter obviously wanted adventure, and *that* was what got him in trouble all the time!

The barber struck a deal with Peter. He would arrange his release, but Peter would have to find berth on a ship. With a three-count prison record, a black boy in New York had little hope of finding employment. But half the crews of sailing ships were black sailors who had taken to the sea for one reason or another.

At that suggestion, Peter looked straight up, and his eyes shone. The sea. It was exactly the thing for him! How often he had thought about just such an adventure as he watched the ships come into Kingston harbor. Now *he* would be one of those sailors, setting out on a long voyage.

When Belle next saw her son, he had new purpose. He was going to sea! Quietly, she listened as he told her all that the barber had done for him. His mentor had found him a berth aboard the ship *Dove* of Nantucket. He would leave within the month.

In the summer of 1839, Belle said goodbye to Peter as he slung a seaman's bag over his shoulder and boarded the *Dove*.

Voyages, in those days, were long—often three, four, or five years. The sailors would write letters and save them until they met a passing ship that was headed for their home port. Then the whole bag of letters was traded from the outgoing to the homebound ship. Months later, the letter would be received by parents, friends, or loved ones anxiously awaiting word.

During the next three years, Belle received three letters from Peter. In the first, Peter called the *Dove* an "unlucky ship," though he did not say why. He inquired about his cousins and sisters, and asked his mother to write to him. "I am your only son, that is so far from your home, in the wide, briny ocean. I have seen more of the world than ever I expected, and if I ever should return home safe, I will tell you all my troubles and hardships."

The letter was dated October 17, 1840.

The next letter came from an island he called Otaheite, among the Society Islands. It was dated March 22, 1841.

And finally, a third letter arrived on September 19, 1841:

"I want to know what sort of a time is at home. We had very bad luck when first we came out; but since we

PETER'S CLIPPER SHIP

have had very good; so I am in hopes to do well yet; but if I don't do well, you need not expect me home these five years. So write as quick as you can, won't you?"

Immediately, as she had done with the first two letters, Belle dictated a reply to her son. She waited to hear more from him.

She never did. The letter of September 1841 was the last she received.

For the rest of her life she would carry those three letters with her. She showed them to anyone who asked what had become of Peter. Always, she waited for the next letter. But it never arrived.

Years later, she heard that the ship *Dove* of Nantucket

had returned to New York Harbor. The seaman known as "Peter Williams" was not aboard. No one knew what had become of him.

During the fourteen years that she was in New York City, Belle worked in many different households. Some of her employers had been associated with the "Kingdom of God," but she left them when she severed her ties with Pierson and his followers. Always a hard worker and strictly honest, Belle received recommendations and high praise from everyone she had worked for.

Her final residence in New York was with the Whiting family on Canal Street. With Peter away at sea and only her church duties and house chores to occupy her, Belle's daily life assumed a steady sameness.

She was now forty-six years old. From time to time news reached her from her daughters; they were growing up, finding husbands. Soon she would have grandchildren.

Working hard as she did, Belle tried once again to save up the money she had lost to the "Kingdom of God." Looking ahead, she saw that steady diligence might eventually earn her clothes, jewelry, or furnishings. It was even possible that she might one day possess a small house of her own.

But what were the rewards for her in owning fine clothes and plush furnishings?

Her experiences in the city left her disillusioned about property and money. Everywhere she turned, someone seemed to be exploiting someone else for the sake of wealth. "Yes," she said to one friend, "the rich rob the poor and the poor rob one another."

She had to ask herself: why remain in the city when she did not *want* wealth and property? It seemed to her that everything she had pursued in New York only led to failure and disappointment.

On the other hand, what were her prospects elsewhere? Who could help her? True, she could start out blindly, hoping for the best. But where was the end of the road for a poor, single black woman who was already considered "old?"

A writer who spoke to Belle in her later years described the dilemma that Belle faced, and the resolution she came to:

> Her decision was that she must leave the city. It was no place for her. She felt called in spirit to travel east and lecture.
>
> She had never been further east than the city. Neither had she any friends outside the city from whom she could expect anything. Yet to her it was plain that her mission lay in the east, and that she would find friends there.
>
> She determined on leaving; but these determinations and convictions she kept close locked in her own breast, knowing that if her children and friends were aware of her intentions, they would make such an ado as would render it very unpleasant, if not distressing to all parties.

Have you ever faced a decision like this? You know there is something that you want to do very strongly, but you cannot say exactly why? Sometimes your impulses are not logical. They can't be explained. A plan gradually forms in your mind. It becomes stronger and stronger every day. Finally, one morning, you wake up with the certainty that you must go ahead with your plan, no matter what happens.

In some respects, Belle's intentions were very clear. She knew that whenever she lectured in a church or meeting, she drew a crowd. When she exhorted people to believe in Jesus and refrain from sin, she did not sound like other ministers who preached. Maybe that was because her message concerned more than religion. She had a way of talking about sin that made people realize it was not just a devil with horns and a pitchfork who corrupted them. It was the unjust ways of their own society.

Along with her warnings, Belle had a powerful message that had grown stronger through the years. When she spoke, she said she "testified to the hope that was in her."

If she did not travel and let her voice be heard, then how would the world hear that message? How could she communicate her urgent hope to people who desperately needed to listen?

So she decided for herself: the time had come! She must travel, testify, and endure whatever hardships her mission entailed.

But just as strongly, Belle felt it was impossible to carry her old name on the new journey that she envisioned for herself. She had been born "Hardenbergh's Belle."

Then she had become "Neely's Belle," "Schryver's Belle," and "Dumont's Belle." Even in New York City she felt as if she was in a "house of bondage." If she was to go out and testify, she needed a name that had never been attached to a slave master of any kind.

She needed a name that a woman could wear with pride, a name that reflected her determination to travel and to speak honestly in her quest for hope.

The first name that came to mind was biblical. "Sojourner." A "sojourner" was a traveler who only rested temporarily, never staying one place too long.

The last name was her creed: "Truth"

She would never rest in one place too long. From this time forward, she would be a sojourner, traveling and testifying. And wherever she went, she would speak the truth, no matter what the consequences.

Her new name would be "Sojourner Truth."

When Belle told Mrs. Whiting that she was leaving to travel east, she declared her new name as well.

Mrs. Whiting was puzzled. Why "Sojourner?" What did this mean? Mrs. Whiting only knew Belle as a quiet, hard worker, with a deep devotion to her faith. Why had this black woman suddenly taken it into her head to travel and testify?

"Why are you going east?" asked Mrs. Whiting, trying to understand the significance of this sudden decision.

"The Spirit calls me there," said Sojourner, "and I must go."

That was all she said, but she said it with such unquestioning conviction that Mrs. Whiting knew that the proud woman could not be deterred.

The next morning before dawn Sojourner Truth slipped a change of clothing into a pillowcase, hooked a basket of food over her arm, and set out for the ferry landing.

On June 1, 1843, as the orange sun cast its glow on the swirling waters of the East River, the steam whistle of the Brooklyn ferry blasted three times. The paddle-wheel began churning.

On the lower deck, crowded among the other black passengers, was a tall woman in a white bonnet with a pillowcase and basket beside her. As the ship headed across the water toward Brooklyn, she gazed steadily to the East.

The extraordinary journey of a woman named Sojourner Truth had just begun.

CHAPTER SEVEN

Testifying

Frederick Douglass

NORTHAMPTON ASSOCIATION

When Sojourner Truth stepped off the ferry onto the Brooklyn Landing, she had exactly two York shillings tucked into the pocket of her long dress. In those days, it was the equivalent of twenty-five cents. That was enough to buy something to eat or perhaps pay for a short ride in a public carriage, but not enough to guarantee a night's lodging at a comfortable inn.

She was taking a very great risk. Can you imagine starting out to cross the country with about two dollars in your pocket?

But Sojourner relied on God's help and the help of others to make her way in the world. She was not setting out to make her fortune. She was setting out to testify what she felt to be God's truth. For that journey, she felt God would provide.

During the first month of her journey, she traveled by foot. At night, she knocked on doors until she found someone who would take her in. She sometimes stayed a few days, doing odd jobs to earn a few shillings so she could go on. But she never remained too long.

What was her destination? Where would she go next? If you had asked her, she could not have told you. She lectured whenever she had the opportunity. She worked whenever she needed to earn a few more shillings. God did not rest, so why should she?

As she explained to someone later in life:

"If God is 'all in all' and 'worketh all in all,' as I have heard them read, then it is impossible He should rest at all; for if he did, every other thing would stop and rest too; the waters would not flow, and the fishes could not swim; and all motion must cease."

Sojourner concluded that God "was to be worshipped at all times and in all places."

Wherever she found a church or a camp meeting or a group of people, she rose to speak. She called these speeches "testifying."

On July 4, 1843, she arrived at Huntington, on the north shore of Long Island. In a nearby town, Cold Springs, a mass temperance meeting was under way. The purpose of the meeting was to ban the sale or drinking of liquor. Numerous leaders spoke against the evils of alcohol, mostly on religious grounds.

Having just come from New York City, Sojourner had seen many examples of drunkenness. She willingly spoke at the meeting. She was invited to stay at Cold Springs for three weeks, while the speeches and prayers continued. During that time, the temperance group lived together in tents or summer houses, sharing their meals and recreation. Their discussions were often heated. Though Sojourner was probably the only black woman, she participated equally in the cooking, speechifying, and other activities.

When it was over, she took a ferry across Long Island Sound to Bridgeport, Connecticut. Turning toward New Haven, she took to the road again, speaking whenever she could, and working when she had to earn money.

For a while she fell in with a religious group called the Adventists, centered near Hartford, Connecticut. They believed that the year 1843 was set aside for Judgment Day. At some moment during that year, they believed, Jesus Christ would come to earth and all the Dead would rise up to be born again. As 1843 drew to a close, the Adventists' fervor became more intense, as they waited with a mixture of expectation and terror for the heavens to open.

Sojourner recalled her bad experience with Elijah Pierson and "the Kingdom of God." She wasn't about to join the fanatical Adventists in their tumultuous preparations for the Second Coming. When she rose to speak to them, she demanded:

"Why are you making such a to-do? Aren't you commanded to 'watch and pray?' You are neither watching nor praying! Go back to your tents without noise or tumult. You are in such a state, the Lord might come, move all through the camp, and go away again—and you would never know it!"

Even though she scolded the Adventists, Sojourner made many friends among them. In fact, one woman said the Adventists "listened eagerly to Sojourner, and drank in all she said." The woman observed:

> When Sojourner rose to speak in their assemblies, her commanding figure and dignified manner hushed every trifler into silence. Her singular and sometimes uncouth modes of expression never provoked a laugh. Often the whole audience was melted into tears by her touching stories. Many were the lessons of wisdom and faith that I was delighted to learn from her.

Sojourner never subscribed to the beliefs of the Adventists. But she found an audience that would listen attentively to her. Sojourner's wisdom leapt across religious boundaries. The story she told was so powerful and moving that people of all faiths were "melted into tears."

When the New England hills began to blaze with colors of autumn, Sojourner Truth had only been on the road for a few months.

Already she had gained a following. People who heard her speak repeated her name to others. Sojourner Truth. Sojourner Truth. It was an odd name, but it was said the woman had odd ways. She never stayed long in one place. In her drab dress and white bonnet, looking younger than her forty-six years, the tall black woman seemed quiet, gentle, and humble. But when she began to speak, something powerful happened. A hush fell over the crowd. People turned and listened. She shocked them. She amused them. One moment they would be laughing wholeheartedly—the next, they were crying.

Again and again, throughout the rest of her life, those who listened to her would try to describe what made her such a powerful speaker.

They would quote her words in long newspaper articles.

They would repeat her phrases in churches and at camp meetings.

They would read the story of her life or buy post-cards with her picture on them.

But no one could convey what it meant to be in the presence of Sojourner Truth when she began to speak or began to sing.

For that very reason, people advised their friends: "Go! Listen to her! You don't want to miss her!"

And no one who took that advice ever forgot the experience.

In the winter of 1843, Sojourner needed a place to live. Some friends she had met on the road introduced her to a group called the Northampton Association of Education and Industry, in Florence, Massachusetts.

The Northampton Association was a utopian community founded by a number of professors, abolitionists, idealists, and workers. The purpose of the community, as stated in its charter, was to "pursue truth, justice, humanity, the equality of rights and rank for all."

Sojourner approved these exalted ideals. At first sight, the community itself did not appeal to her. The three-story structure that housed the Association was a plain, dingy, brick factory building that resembled every other grim, New England mill. Everyone lived together and worked in the same building.

On the ground floor were whirling silk-making machines. In back were bunks for single men. The second floor had a kitchen, a long dining hall, a community store, and a room where women and girls skeined and packed silk. Families lived behind crude partitions on part of the second floor, or upstairs in cubicles on the third floor.

The first night she stayed with the Northampton Association, Sojourner was shown around and introduced to the other boarders by George Benson, one of the founders. She joined the men, women, and children in the main dining room for a supper of salty codfish and soggy potatoes. Then she was shown to a tiny cubicle up on the third floor.

Next morning before dawn she was wakened by a clanging breakfast bell. Babies were howling. By the time she came into the dining room, it was already crowded. The first group of women ate quickly, then hurried off to the silk-making machines.

Sojourner wondered how long she could bear to live in a dull, dreary place like this.

She stayed three years.

What kept her there was certainly not the living conditions or the factory life. Nor was it religion—for the community combined all faiths, and quite a few members were nonbelievers.

Instead, she was drawn by the idealism and openness of the people who seemed to share a common purpose, yet constantly debated the best means of achieving their goals. Later on, someone who visited the Northampton Association would call it "a community composed of some of the choicest spirits of the age, where there was equality of feeling, a liberty of thought and speech, and a largeness of soul."

The Northampton Association had many visitors, and some of them were the most outstanding leaders of the abolitionist cause. The most frequent visitor was probably William Lloyd Garrison. He was a balding, distinguished-looking man with high cheekbones and tiny wire-rimmed spectacles. As the fiery editor of *The Liberator*, he was the most visible abolitionist in the United States. As the cousin of co-founder George Benson, Garrison had come very close to joining the community himself.

He had many other activities. Twelve years before, Garrison had organized the New England Anti-Slavery Society. When Sojourner met him, the untiring editor had just launched the American Anti-Slavery Society.

Everywhere he spoke, Garrison railed against an inhumane and evil system. The masthead of his newspaper blared out: "NO UNION WITH SLAVEHOLDERS!" Aroused to fury, he hurled his judgments in the face of all listeners. Pro slavery crowds shouted him down and threatened to lynch him.

"Prejudice against color is a rebellion against God!" he roared. "The Constitution is a covenant with death and an agreement with hell!"

To Garrison, any Constitution that permitted slavery was not worth the paper it was written on. *The Liberator* openly supported those who defied a law that treated people as property. He applauded the courageous Underground Railway that helped Southern slaves escape to freedom in the North. Let every humane citizen shrug at the law, he said. Let them open their doors to runaway slaves! He believed that everyone, white and black, should defy the law when the law was *wrong*.

Garrison was jailed for publishing his views. He was often threatened by howling mobs. But he never backed down!

Most remarkable of all was the reach of his angry cry. The circulation of *The Liberator* was actually quite small. It never printed more than three thousand copies. Yet Garrison's angry voice could be heard in every corner of the North and South.

When she met Garrison, Sojourner also met a number of passionately committed people who frequently debated him on the antislavery issue. All believed that slavery was wrong, but they disagreed about the means for ending it.

Most prominent was Frederick Douglass, a fugitive slave who had defied and then fled a brutal slave trainer. Many had felt a chill along their spines when they saw

William Lloyd Garrison

the scorn in his lidded glance. With jet black beard and awesome mane of hair framing his dark bronze features, Douglass could be fearsome when his fury was aroused. His anger once caused a slave master to cower, and when it was turned on the system he abhorred, the very heavens seemed to tremble.

Whenever Douglass came to visit the Northampton Association, he spent time with the well-loved Dave "Doc" Ruggles, a blind, black man who had once led the New York Vigilance Committee. Doc had helped dozens of slaves in their flight along the Underground Railway. Frederick Douglass was among those he had saved from recapture.

After he lost his eyesight, Ruggles could no longer

work as a doctor. He had no place to live and no one to care for him. As a representative of the Northampton Association, George Benson had gone to New York City and invited Ruggles to become a permanent member of the Association. Ruggles had been there ever since.

Although Sojourner Truth met many other abolitionists at the community, these three above all challenged her, stimulated her thinking, and opened her eyes. She had learned a great deal through her personal experience. Men like Garrison, Douglass and Ruggles gave her another kind of education.

From Douglass she learned the power of the printed word. She was still illiterate. She could not read a syllable of *The Liberator* that Garrison kept tucked under his arm. When others in the community read from its pages, as they did every week, she was amazed at what had been written. Only the Bible had so moved her with its truthfulness!

Douglass presented another kind of challenge. Sojourner had always been a woman of peace. She used her voice to calm crowds. She forgave the slaveholder. In fact, she pitied the slaveholder. She felt in her heart that every slaveholder would suffer damnation for the evils he committed on earth.

Douglass was not so gentle with his words and judgments. Sometimes when he spoke, it was from a brooding sense of despair. Sojourner wanted to challenge him. She wanted to "testify her *hope!*"

Yet she had trouble raising her voice against Douglass. Here was a black man with experiences even more terrible than hers. He preached that there was no victory in submission. Douglass had turned on his white tormentor and forced him to yield.

Now he was called "the black hero" of the abolitionist cause. He was the first black to serve the Massachusetts Anti-Slavery Society as a full-time agent. When Sojourner met him, Douglass at age twenty-six was well read and politically aware. Perhaps there was more truth in his raging despair than in all her quiet hope. Who was she to challenge the views he passionately held?

With Doc Ruggles, Sojourner felt no such inward struggle. When she first came to the community, Sojourner had wondered about the blind, black man wandering in the midst of white people who respected him and took care of him. Each week, when she brought him his fresh laundry, she heard more of the stories he was telling the children. She realized that his days and nights in New York had been filled with terror—not for himself, but for the slaves he had helped toward freedom. He had faced that terror and won over it by quiet persistence.

For Doc Ruggles the answer was neither hope nor despair, but steadfast determination in the face of all obstacles.

Sojourner Truth remained with the Northampton Association until that grim day in November 1846, when George Benson announced that the community was bankrupt. The silk business, its main enterprise, was not profitable enough to support the idealists who had worked so hard to make their model community a success.

In those three years, something changed deeply in Sojourner Truth. She no longer viewed herself as a lonely traveler. Hers was not a single, isolated voice. There were others in this country who felt as she did. They were working hard to challenge the laws and bring about change.

Like her, they let their inward voices lead them step by step on their journeys. Some would go blind. Others would be thrown in prison. Still others would be attacked by howling mobs.

The atmosphere was filled with danger. When you spoke against slavery, you faced powerful men who considered slaves their possessions. To them, the end of slavery meant highway robbery!

But the people Sojourner met at the Association would let nothing stand in their way. If abolishing slavery meant robbing the slave masters, then they were proud to be called thieves!

A movement was in motion, ready to transform the nation. Sojourner Truth, an illiterate black woman who stepped off the ferry with two York shillings in her pocket, was part of the sweeping tide of change.

CHAPTER EIGHT

Women Are Equal!

Lucretia Mott
Lucy Stone

WOMEN BEHIND PLOWS

I n 1845, the year before the Northampton Association of Education and Industry disbanded, Frederick Douglass published his autobiography, *Narrative of the Life of Frederick Douglass*. Among abolitionists it was an immediate bestseller. But for Douglass the publication meant trouble. The *Narrative* revealed in print that he was a runaway slave.

Under the existing Fugitive Slave Law, first passed in 1793, Douglass was a fugitive who could be arrested and tried at any time. To escape a prolonged trial, he took a ship to England. (He was not to return until 1847, when English friends purchased his freedom.)

Douglass's narrow escape was on Sojourner's mind when a friend of hers, Olive Gilbert, offered to write her memoirs. William Lloyd Garrison was enthusiastic. Of course he would publish it! He could see the *Narrative of Sojourner Truth* taking its place alongside the *Narrative of the Life of Frederick Douglass* in every bookstore around the country!

Despite the risk, Sojourner agreed to work with Olive Gilbert. When the Association broke up, a small house was built for her by Sam Hill, a friend of George Benson and co-founder of the Association. In payment for the house, Sojourner signed a promissory note for three hundred dollars. She placed an "X" on the document as her signature. She had planned to pay most of it by cooking and cleaning for George Benson and other citizens of Northampton. But if she had a book to sell, she could pay off the note that much faster!

It was 1850 before Sojourner held the first bound copy in her hand. She could not read a single word of it. But there was no mistaking the simple, etched portrait in the front of the book. This was a book about her. It was the story of her own life!

The next time she saw Olive Gilbert, her high spirits plummeted. Olive had bad news. None of the bookstores would carry Sojourner's *Narrative*.

The reaction to Douglass and the abolitionists was being felt all over the country. Proslavery forces smashed windows, howled at abolitionist speakers, and burned effigies of antislavery leaders. These mobs were bloodthirsty. They clamored for stricter Fugitive Slave Laws.

Carrying shotguns loaded with birdshot, with baying hounds on the scent, they stalked the dusty roads and the Carolina swamps to kidnap slaves and drag them back to the plantations.

Who wanted to carry the slim memoirs of an aging black woman who condemned slavery as "a soul-killing system?" No doubt about it, this *Narrative* was strong medicine. Sojourner Truth and Olive Gilbert did not mince words when they declared:

> Slaveholders expect us to listen to their horror of ideas. But we know how calmly and quietly they contemplate the present state of licentiousness their own wicked laws have created—not only as it regards the slave, but as it regards the more privileged portion of the population of the South.

Such words would inflame Southern plantation owners, Northern slave traders and all those secretly or openly sympathetic to the cause of the South. The seeds of the Civil War were already being sown. No scholarly minded bookstore owner wanted to risk being caught in the fire by selling the *Narrative of Sojourner Truth*.

Sojourner did not hesitate to take action. Packing her carpetbag with copies of her *Narrative*, she set out on the road to sell the book herself. In 1851 she traveled to Worcester, where she attended the first national Women's Rights Convention. The meeting drew many antislavery advocates, including Frederick Douglass and William Lloyd Garrison.

To Sojourner, many of the women's complaints at the Rights Convention seemed very distant from her own concerns. Lucretia Mott, a prim, tiny woman wearing a lacy bonnet, talked about being a teacher. She was outraged that she was only paid half as much as the men who worked alongside her. Lucy Stone, a young, eloquent graduate of Oberlin College, announced that she would never take a man's name as her own. She said she would not allow a man to have rights over any of her possessions.

Sojourner knew what it was like to have no rights and no possessions. She listened keenly to the women who rose confidently to speak. But then she grew impatient: "Sisters, I'm not clear what you be after. If women want any rights more than they've got, why don't they just take them and not be talking about it."

As the discussions continued, she realized that the issues were not so easily settled. To Sojourner, and to many abolitionists at that meeting, the antislavery cause had much in common with the women's rights movement. Their voices were united when they called out for freedom, dignity, and equality, regardless of race or sex.

After the Worcester meetings, Sojourner returned for a short time to Northampton. She did not stay for long. Garrison wanted her to travel and speak with George Thompson, an English abolitionist on tour. In

George Thompson

February 1851, Sojourner met Thompson in Springfield, a day's travel from Northampton. Angry mobs had heard that George Thompson was coming to the city. That night in the main square, three effigies were torched. They represented William Lloyd Garrison, George Thompson, and John Bull, the symbol of England.

As the flaming effigies lit the night sky and the gesturing men shouted themselves hoarse, Sojourner realized what she would face on her next journey. Everywhere she looked, there was hatred. Yet the more hatred she saw, the more certain she was that her journey should continue.

To Sojourner's disappointment, Garrison was unable to go on the speaking tour. His newspaper business was too urgent. Thompson offered to pay all Sojourner's expenses if she would accompany him. She readily agreed.

The two spoke in Union City, Little Falls, West Winfield, Peterboro, and many other towns throughout western Massachusetts and northern New York State. In his precise, upper-class British accent, George Thompson appealed to people's reason. Calling upon their sense of fair play and justice, he reminded them of principles of freedom and equality. These principles were declared in their own Declaration of Independence!

But it was Sojourner who gripped the crowd. When it was her turn to speak, she often astonished listeners by bursting into song:

> *I am pleading for my people—*
> *A poor, downtrodden race,*
> *Who dwell in freedom's boasted land*
> *With no abiding place.*
>
> *I am pleading for the mothers*
> *Who gaze in wild despair*
> *Upon the hated auction block*
> *And see their children there.*
>
> *I plead with you to sympathize*
> *With sighs and groans and scars,*
> *And note how base the tyranny*
> *Beneath the stripes and stars.*

They were words she had composed herself—a battle hymn that called people to sympathize with the oppressed rather than go to war. When she followed the song with her simple, forceful speech, the audience was mesmerized.

In Rochester, New York, George Thompson and Sojourner parted ways. Thompson headed north to Canada, where he continued lecturing against slavery. Sojourner moved in with a Quaker family, Amy and Isaac Post, who lived on Sophia Street a short distance from Frederick Douglass. Ever since his return from England in 1847, Douglass had been publishing his own antislavery paper, *The North Star*. Whenever Sojourner was scheduled to speak, announcements appeared in the *Star*.

Rochester was a strategic location on the Underground Railway route. Often, escaped slaves making their way North slept in the Posts' barn. Late at night, a curtained carriage would transport them to the city docks. From there they were smuggled aboard boats bound for Canada—and freedom!

In those days, anyone offering help to escaped slaves could be fined and imprisoned, and the slaves would be sent back to certain punishment. Fortunately the Posts were surrounded by many who were sympathetic to their beliefs. It is likely that their neighbors knew about the slaves hidden in the barn. People on Sophia Street certainly suspected that the Post house was a stopping point on the Underground Railway. But their neighbors never broke the unwritten code of silence.

In May of 1851, Sojourner boarded a steamer for Detroit. From there she traveled to Akron, Ohio, where she was asked to speak at a Women's Rights Convention. The distinguished writer and humanitarian who presided over the convention was Frances D. Gage, who later described the meeting in an antislavery journal.

At first, the meeting was dominated by Methodist, Baptist, Episcopal, Presbyterian, and Universalist ministers who had come to heckle the women working for social reform. During their speeches, several of the men said they were entitled to superior rights and privileges because they had "superior intellect." They also claimed spiritual superiority because Jesus Christ was a man.

Frances Gage told her readers what happened after the men had their say:

Then, slowly from her seat in the corner rose Sojourner Truth, who, till now, had scarcely lifted her head. She moved solemnly to the front, laid her old bonnet at her feet, and turned her great speaking eyes on me.

There was a hissing sound of disapprobation above and below. I rose and announced, "Sojourner Truth," and begged the audience to keep silence for a few moments.

The tumult subsided at once, and every eye was fixed on this almost Amazon form, which stood nearly six feet high, head erect and eyes piercing the upper air like one in a dream. At her first word there was a profound hush. She spoke in deep tones, which, though not loud, reached every ear in the house and away through the doors and windows:

"Well, children, where there is so much racket, there

must be something out of kilter. That man over there says that women need to be helped into carriages and lifted over ditches—and to have the best place everywhere. Nobody ever helps me into carriages or over mud-puddles—or gives me the best place at the table!"

Raising herself to her full height, and lifting her voice to a pitch like rolling thunder, Sojourner asked, "And ain't I a woman? Look at me! Look at my arm!" (She bared her right arm to the shoulder, showing her tremendous muscular power.) "I have ploughed and planted and gathered into barns, and no man could get ahead of me! And ain't I a woman?

"I could work as much and eat as much as a man—when I could get it—and bear the lash as well! And ain't I a woman?

"My mother bore ten children and saw them sold off to slavery, and when I cried with my mother's grief, none but Jesus heard me! And ain't I a woman?

"Then that little man in black says women can't have as many rights as men. If the first woman God ever made was strong enough to turn the world upside down all alone, these women together" (and she glanced over the platform) "ought to be able to turn it back and get it right side up again! And now that the women are asking to do it, the men better let 'em."

Long-continued cheering greeted this.

"I'm obliged to you for hearing me," she concluded, "and now old Sojourner hasn't got nothing more to say."

Amid roars of applause, she returned to her corner, leaving more than one of us with streaming eyes and hearts beating with gratitude. She had taken us up in her strong arms and carried us safely over the slough of difficulty, turning the whole tide in our favor.

I have never in my life seen anything like the magical influence that subdued the mobbish spirit of the day and turned the sneers and jeers of an excited crowd into notes of respect and admiration. Hundreds rushed up to shake hands with her and congratulate the glorious old mother, and bid her Godspeed on her mission of "testifying again concerning the wickedness of this-here people."

CHAPTER NINE

Prelude to War

Dred Scott

RIOTS

As we look back in American history, the Civil War may now seem inevitable to us. How could the institution of slavery continue? How could a nation founded on principles of liberty allow human beings to be treated like cattle?

But neither Sojourner Truth nor any others of her time could foresee the War that was coming. The most visionary observed powerful historical forces clashing. Many said that war and bloodshed were inevitable. It was a bleak prospect. If the nation was divided down the middle, North and South might never again be reunited.

From 1851 up to the outbreak of the Civil War in 1861, Sojourner Truth was tossed about in the raging controversy. The war against slavery blazed first in speeches, in print, in riots, in legislative hearings, court cases, lynchings, beatings, and assassinations before it burst into full-fledged war.

In 1850, when Sojourner was still in Massachusetts, Congress had endorsed an appalling decision—to reinforce and broaden the scope of the 1793 Fugitive Slave Law. According to the new version of the law passed in 1850, "all good citizens" were commanded to return fugitive slaves to Federal marshals. Fugitives could be hauled before a Federal commissioner and thrown back to their slave masters without the benefit of a trial.

In 1854 came the Kansas-Nebraska Act, another setback for antislavery forces and a victory for slave owners. Although not flatly stated in the Act, slavery was the real issue. It said, let the settlers in a new state decide whether that state should be a slave state or a free state. Everyone knew that Kansas would become a slave state if the slave owning citizens were allowed to decide for themselves, which is exactly what happened.

It was the year 1857 that delivered the most horrendous miscarriage of justice. Dred Scott, a Negro slave, had been taken into free territory by his master. The slave had refused to return home with his master, claiming his freedom. The Supreme Court ruled that Scott would have to remain a slave. Three esteemed justices of the Court said that "any Negro whose ancestors were sold as slaves" was not entitled to the rights of a Federal citizen. Ex-slaves had no stand in court! The greatest legal minds in the United States had decided that black people were invisible in the eyes of the law!

Each piece of legislation and each narrow court decision was like a battering ram that threatened to sink a fragile ship of liberty. As Southern slave owners and pro-slavery forces gathered momentum, the pleas of abolitionists and antislavery advocates began to sound more despairing. They knew they were right, but what could they do when Congress, the courts, and the Federal law were all against them?

Throughout those years, Sojourner Truth moved restlessly about the country, listening, testifying, searching for answers, declaring what she saw as the truth, raising her voice in hymns, songs, and speeches. Everywhere she traveled she carried the *Narrative of Sojourner Truth*. Her listeners clamored to buy a copy. Six hundred copies of the *Narrative* were sent to her by Garrison. She carried them from town to town in the baggage compartment of a buggy that had been loaned to her by friends in Salem, Ohio.

When the first edition was sold out, her supporters arranged for a second printing.

She also sold copies of her songs, asking a few cents for each one. What she received from sale of her books and songs was very little. But it was enough to support her so that she could reach the next town, the next assembly, and raise her voice again.

At this time she also carried a few possessions that became her trademarks. Her pipe was always with her. Ever since her days as a slave girl on the Ulster County farms, she had enjoyed smoking tobacco. Though she herself disapproved of the habit, it was not until many years later that she was able to give it up.

Now in her fifties, she also carried a cane. People said she needed the cane to ward off angry mobs, but it wasn't true. After all the walking she had done in her lifetime, she had begun to feel some weakness in her knees. The cane helped. She was grateful to be able to travel by horse and buggy rather than on foot.

Often, she had no destination in mind when she set out in the morning. When she came to a crossroads on a lonely stretch of Ohio roads, she would drop the reins on the horse's neck. Let the horse be guided! When he started off in one direction, she would pick up the reins and continue driving again.

Wherever she ended up, she would attract a crowd with her singing, then hold a meeting. Afterwards, someone saw to it that her horse was fed and watered. Lodging was never a problem. Once people had heard her speak, they clamored for the privilege of having the tall, black woman spend the night in their homes.

A man living near Mt. Pleasant, Iowa, vividly recalled how she appeared and spoke in those days:

> This unlearned African woman, with her deep religious and trustful nature burning in her soul like fire, has an astounding, magnetic power over an audience. I was once present in a religious meeting where some speaker had alluded to the government of the United States and had uttered sentiments in favor of its Constitution.

Sojourner stood erect and tall with her white turban on her head, and in a low and subdued voice began by saying:

"Children, I talk to God and God talks to me. I go out and talk to God in the fields and in the woods. This morning I was walking out, and I got over the fence. I saw the wheat a-holding up its head, looking very big. I went up and I took hold of it. You believe it—there was *no* wheat there! I said, 'God, what *is* the matter with this wheat?' And He said to me, 'Sojourner, there is a little weevil in it.'

"Now I hear talking about the Constitution and the rights of man. I come up and I take hold of this Constitution. It looks *mighty big*, but when I feel for *my* rights, there ain't any there. Then I say, 'God what *ails* this Constitution?'

"He says to me, 'Sojourner, there is a little *weevil* in it!' "

A weevil in the Constitution! To the farmers of the Midwest, this image had clear meaning. The weevil had destroyed thousands of acres of wheat crops. The "weevil" in the Constitution was just as damaging, because the Constitution permitted slavery—and slavery was eating away at the nation!

When Sojourner heard small-mindedness or bigotry, she could not keep silent. She exploded with indignation. No one who witnessed her moments of wrath ever forgot the experience.

At one meeting she had to endure the speech of a

petty lawyer who said "colored people" were just like "monkeys, baboons, and orangutans." As his long, drawling speech drew to a close, Sojourner stepped up to the platform. Suddenly she straightened to her full height. Someone in the audience recalled her exact words:

"Children, I am one of the monkey tribes. I was born a slave. I had the dirty work to do—the scullion work."

She pointed her long, bony finger with withering scorn at the petty lawyer.

"In the course of my time I have done a great deal of dirty scullion work, but of all the dirty work I ever did, cleaning up after this man is the scullionest and the dirtiest."

Too frequently, Sojourner had dirty work of this kind to do. But she also had a task even more difficult— trying to bring hope to those who were losing it. Frederick Douglass, for one.

For Douglass, the 1850 Fugitive Slave Law was like a knife-stab in his own heart. To him it meant the slave masters were winning! All across the North, Federal marshals were on the prowl for slaves fleeing the South. They lurked at borders between slave and nonslave states, waiting to pounce upon frightened men, trembling children, and women with babies in their arms.

At one meeting Douglass attacked Northerners and Southerners who profited from human misery. He spoke with despair of the thousands of black men, women, and children who had tried to cross the Ohio River in their flight to Canada. He had seen them hunted down in the fields and forests, shackled together, and herded back to the South.

As he spoke, Douglass's voice took on a note of rage. "There is no longer any hope for justice other than bloody rebellion," he cried. "Slavery must end in blood!"

The crowd was stunned. Here was a black man calling for whites to be murdered in retribution for their crimes against humanity.

Even for the abolitionists, that was going too far. They wanted justice and equality, not a bloodbath.

Here was Douglass, a thoughtful man dedicated to his cause, advocating a policy of retaliation. Was this a signal of what was to come?

Sojourner rose to her feet and pointed her finger at the famous editor of *The North Star*.

"Frederick," she demanded, "is God dead?"

"No," he answered at once. "And because God is not dead, slavery can only end in blood."

Sojourner did not share his vision.

But Douglass's words would prove prophetic.

Sojourner's travels during the years before the Civil War took her from Ohio to Michigan and other Midwestern states, then east again to Ulster County, to various parts of Massachusetts, and finally back to Michigan again.

What drew her to Michigan was a small, converted barn on College Street behind Charles Merritt's house in the town of Battle Creek. For Sojourner, this barn was her new home.

Though Sojourner had purchased a small house near Northampton, Massachusetts, she never considered it a permanent home. She had paid off the promissory note to Mr. Hill. The little house in Massachusetts belonged to her. But for some reason, she felt much more comfortable far away in Battle Creek, Michigan.

She was first drawn to the small Michigan town in 1856, when she went there to attend a Friends of Human Progress meeting. Afterwards, she was often welcomed to the tables of Quakers like the Merritts and other antislavery sympathizers. Battle Creek was a center of abolitionism, where Fugitive Slave Laws were openly defied. Fleeing slaves felt so secure in Battle Creek that some had set up shacks at the end of College Street.

Sojourner could have stayed with many families in town, but the furnished barn was comfortable. Already she had plans to make over the barn into a real house. But she was so busy traveling and speaking that she had no time to begin renovations.

Yet it was a place to return to. Whenever she needed help or wanted company, there were friends nearby.

She dreamed of one day having all her family together in Battle Creek. Throughout the years, she had sometimes written to her daughters when someone could take dictation from her.

Diana, Elizabeth and Sophia had been legally freed when each of them reached the age of nineteen. They had stayed on with Dumont for awhile, continuing to work for wages after they were freed. But eventually all three moved away and married.

At some time—it is not known exactly when—the three daughters moved to Battle Creek or the nearby town of Harmonia to be near their mother. Elizabeth had been married twice, first to a man named Caldwell, who died leaving her a widow, and then to a man with the last name of Banks. She had one son, James Caldwell, by her first husband, and a second son, Sammy Banks, by her second.

Diana married Jacob Corbin, a hotel cook in Battle Creek, and their son Frank Corbin frequently stayed with Sojourner. Sophia's son William Boyd was the same age as Frank, and the two boys often played together when they came to visit their grandmother.

Sammy Banks, who was twelve years older than Frank and William, came to know his grandmother very well. Bright and always active, Sammy accompanied Sojourner as she went about her chores, doing housework, nursing the sick, and caring for children. When Sojourner sold blackberries gathered from the Merritts' garden, Sammy ran ahead and announced that his grandmother was coming right behind with "nice, fresh, ripe berries."

They became a well-known sight in the town—the towering woman with the basket of fruit on her head, and the skinny, noisy boy who dashed ahead of her. Sojourner had a special reason for taking great pride in her grandson. Sammy was learning to read!

On April 13, 1861, an excited boy rushed up to his grandmother's house waving a copy of Battle Creek's

newspaper. Carefully he pronounced the single bold word printed in huge black type on the front of the paper: "WAR!!" The previous day, Sammy read slowly, a Confederate general had fired on Fort Sumter.

The Civil War had begun!

CHAPTER TEN

Words for Lincoln

President Abraham Lincoln

REGIMENT OF BLACK SOLDIERS

s armed hostilities flared, the war of words also continued.

In the fall of 1862, Sojourner Truth accompanied the fierce feminist and antislavery advocate, Josephine Griffing, on a dangerous journey to Indiana.

A law had just been passed banning all blacks from the state. Sojourner, with Josephine at her side, openly defied the law by speaking in public. Angry mobs threatened to throw her in jail. Indiana citizens cried out "Nigger! Nigger!" They threatened to burn the town house where she was to appear. She declared, "Then I will speak upon the ashes."

In Indiana, Sojourner won many men over to her side. When she marched to the Angola courthouse, dressed in a red, white, and blue shawl, with stars on her hat and shoulders, she was escorted by double files of soldiers with arms presented.

But proslavery sympathizers were everywhere. "At all of our meetings," Josephine Griffing recalled, "we were told that armed men were in our midst and had declared that they would blow out our brains."

By the time Sojourner left Indiana for Battle Creek, she had won thousands over to her side. During that time, she had been terrorized and threatened by people who spewed hatred. The strain took its toll. The cause that had taken her through half a dozen states, to hundreds of large cities and small towns, across thousands of miles of country roads, had finally left her exhausted.

In the winter of 1862, she fell ill. She was sixty-five years old, and some of her closest friends doubted that she would recover again. There were rumors that Sojourner was dying.

In April of 1863, the fame of Sojourner Truth increased—but so did the rumors of her death.

The cause of both was publication of an article in the *Atlantic Monthly* by Harriet Beecher Stowe, the author of *Uncle Tom's Cabin*. In the *Atlantic* article, Mrs. Stowe declared, "Sojourner Truth has passed away from among us . . . but her memory still lives."

Mrs. Stowe was mistaken. Sojourner was very much alive. However, it was true that she was very ill.

Close at Sojourner's side during her weeks as an invalid was a Battle Creek friend, Mrs. Phebe H. M. Stick-

Harriet Beecher Stowe

ney. Partly to squelch the rumor of Sojourner's death, Mrs. Stickney wrote a strong letter to the *National Anti-Slavery Standard*. She told of Sojourner's condition and appealed for funds.

Many *Standard* readers had been at Sojourner's side when she spoke and welcomed her into their homes. The response to Mrs. Stickney's message was a wave of contributions from points as distant as Iowa, Massachusetts, New York, and even Ireland. Along with the money came praise for Sojourner's past work.

"This extraordinary woman still lives!" rejoiced one reader. "Few, if any, in the land are more worthy of our contributions. Here has been a life of preeminent devotion to the sacred cause of liberty and purity."

The outpouring of good feeling was like a strong medicine to Sojourner. Along the miles she had traveled, Sojourner had forged a community of like-minded individuals. Though many were advocates of different causes, they shared their belief in a common goal. Each felt great friendship for the proud woman who had always spoken her mind.

"You see, child," Sojourner explained to Mrs. Stickney, "when you wrote that letter you didn't think you were doing much. But I tell you, dear lamb, when a thing is done in the right spirit, God takes it up and spreads it all over the country."

Far from Battle Creek, the Civil War had entered its bleakest hours as the Union lost battle. Then gradually, through the winter of 1862, the tide began to turn. On January 1, 1863, Abraham Lincoln shook the nation by signing the Emancipation Proclamation.

It was a document he had written and rewritten many times, until every word conveyed the full weight of his momentous decision:

All persons held as slaves within any state or designated part of a state, the people whereof shall then be in rebellion against the United States, shall be then, henceforward and forever free.

From that moment on, every slave in the Confederacy had the legal right, proclaimed by the President of the United States, to walk away from his or her master.

Coming just after the battle of Antietam, the Proclamation had a liberating effect on the spirit of the Union. In Rochester, New York, Frederick Douglass wrote: "The effect of the announcement was startling beyond description, and the scene was wild and grand. Joy and gladness exhausted all forms of expression, from shouts of praise to sobs and tears."

Shortly after the signing of the Proclamation, Lincoln gave the order to recruit Negro troops to fight for the Union. Sojourner's grandson, James Caldwell, signed up with the all-Negro 54th Massachusetts Regiment. By June, he was marching alongside hundreds of black soldiers. In Union blue, with banners flying, the first black Regiment drilled on Boston Common.

Sojourner listened with pride as Sammy read news of the 54th from the pages of the *National Anti-Slavery Standard.*

Each day she was feeling better. "I've budded out with the trees," she told a friend, as the warmth of spring nurtured her own returning health. She began working again, cleaning, washing clothes, selling fresh berries . . . and anxiously awaiting news of the "great war."

When a photographer came to town, Sojourner asked him to take her picture. For the portrait she was seated next to a small table holding a cut glass vase of flowers, with a book on the table, and some knitting in her hands. Wire-rimmed spectacles clung to the bridge of her nose, and a white, fringed shawl was draped around her shoulders.

Sojourner had the portrait made into postcards.

Under her picture was printed the inscription, "The Shadow supports the Substance." It was her own way of saying, "Buy this postcard, and help support my work."

The *National Anti-Slavery Standard* willingly printed the announcement that "a card photograph of that noble woman, Sojourner Truth, is available to the public."

Now, more than a hundred years since they were printed, Sojourner Truth can still be seen in the fading, brown-tinted postcards that people saved to remember her. She gazes out of the picture with serious eyes, a witness to the great events of her century.

During the autumn of 1863, the Michigan Regiment of Colored Soldiers was stationed in Detroit, a hundred miles from Battle Creek. Sojourner decided to bring the troops Thanksgiving dinner. Around Battle Creek she knocked on doors, stopped pedestrians, and spoke in churches, collecting donations from anyone who would listen.

On Thanksgiving Day she arrived in front of Colonel Bennett's quarters at Camp Ward. Her wagon groaned with the weight of roasted turkeys, squash, pumpkins, potatoes, carrots, rhutabagas, nuts, fruit cakes, pies, and candies. In an instant, she was surrounded by black soldiers who helped "Aunty Sojourner" down from her perch on the plank wagon seat.

Stepping from his quarters, Colonel Bennett called for dress order and the regiment fell into line. What would Aunty Sojourner have to say to them? It didn't take them long to find out. As one man described it, Sojourner "gave a speech glowing with patriotism and good wishes, which met with rounds of enthusiastic cheers."

After the ceremony, she spent several hours talking to the soldiers, opening boxes and distributing the Thanksgiving feast. Then she led them in a new song composed expressly for the First Michigan Regiment. To the tune of "John Brown's Body," hundreds of voices joined Sojourner Truth in the verses:

We are the valiant soldiers who've 'listed for the war;
We are fighting for the Union, we are fighting for the law;
We can shoot a rebel farther than a white man ever saw, As
we go marching on . . .

Father Abraham has spoken, and the message has been sent;
The prison doors have opened, and out the prisoners went
To join the sable army of African descent,
As we go marching on . . .

Looking among the faces lifted in song, she could not help but think of her own dear grandson, James Caldwell, in the all-Negro 54th Massachusetts Regiment. Just three months before, on August 8, 1863, the courageous regiment had launched a disastrous attack on Fort Wagner in South Carolina. Six hundred fifty had been killed in the first charge.

James Caldwell was listed as missing in action.

There had been no word of him since.

For the soldiers at Camp Ward, Thanksgiving

100

brought good news that helped offset the Fort Wagner disaster. Lincoln's sturdy, brilliant, hard-drinking general, Ulysses S. Grant, had joined Generals William T. Sherman and Joseph Hooker in driving the Confederates back to Georgia.

In March, 1864, Lincoln brought Grant east to become his commander in chief. Two months later, Grant led the Army of the Potomac across the Rapidan River to attack Robert E. Lee. It was the beginning of a long campaign of the bloodiest fighting of the War.

To Sojourner Truth living in Battle Creek, the strategies of War seemed far away. But she sensed that it was a critical time for the nation. Abraham Lincoln, the great man who had emancipated the slaves, needed the help and prayers of every American.

Why shouldn't she, Sojourner Truth, go speak with him?

There was nothing she could tell Abraham Lincoln that he did not already know. But she could offer him the strength of her faith and the encouragement of her words for the trials that lay ahead.

One morning, Sojourner informed Mrs. Merritt that the neatly kept barn in her backyard would be vacant for a while. Sojourner Truth, with her grandson Sammy, was leaving to talk to Mr. Lincoln.

The next morning, she was gone.

For Sojourner the trip across the country was, in some ways, a journey of triumph. From Detroit to Chicago, from Akron to Rochester, and on to New York

City, she saw many friends she had left behind years before. Those who had been saddened by the rumors of her death were overjoyed to see her again.

All who had struggled together in the cause now sensed that they would win at last. The Emancipation Proclamation had been the breath of hope. They were horrified by the slaughter of a modern war fought with repeating rifles and explosive artillery shells. But they had no doubt that their side would win. Now that Lincoln had found Grant to be his general, who could stop the Union?

This time, when she traveled, Sojourner carried a new volume with her. Bound in heavy leather, its pages were mostly blank. Sojourner filled those pages as she went along by asking all those she met to sign their names. She called this volume her "Book of Life."

This time, too, she had a constant companion on her trip, her grandson Sammy. He usually brought meals or arranged the sleeping quarters for his sixty-seven-year-old grandmother. Sojourner was proud that Sammy could read and write, and she made the best use of his talents. When he was not reading the Bible to her, he would bring her up to date with her correspondence. When Sojourner dictated a reply, Sammy transcribed it in his careful, neat handwriting.

Sojourner arrived in Washington early in the fall 1864, but it was late October before she could arrange an introduction to the president. Later, she would remember every detail. For the benefit of her friends, she dictated a description of that momentous occasion:

It was about 8 A.M. when I called on the president. Upon entering his reception room my companion said to him, "This is Sojourner Truth, who has come all the way from Michigan to see you."

He arose, gave me his hand, made a bow, and said, "I am pleased to see you."

I said to him, "Mr. President, when you first took your seat I feared you would be torn to pieces, for I likened you unto Daniel, who was thrown into the lion's den. But I said if God spared you, I would see you before the four years expired."

Then I said, "I appreciate you, for you are the best president who has ever taken the seat."

He replied, "I expect you have reference to my having emancipated the slaves in my proclamation. But George Washington was just as good, and would have done just as I have done if the time had come. If the people on the other side of the Potomac River had behaved themselves, I could not have done what I have. But they did not, which gave me the opportunity to do these things."

I then said, "I thank God that you were the instrument selected by Him and the people to do it."

I must say, and I am proud to say, that I never was treated by any one with more kindness and cordiality than were shown to me by that great and good man, Abraham Lincoln, by the grace of God president of the United States for four years more.

He took my little "Book of Life" and with the same hand that signed the death-warrant of slavery, he wrote as follows:

"For Aunty Sojourner Truth,
Oct. 29, 1864. A. LINCOLN"

As I was taking my leave, he arose and took my hand and said he would be pleased to have me call again. I felt that I was in the presence of a friend, and I now thank God from the bottom of my heart that I always have advocated his cause and have done it openly and boldly. I shall feel still more in duty bound to do so in time to come. May God assist me.

The letter was addressed from Freedman's Village in Arlington Heights, Virginia. At that time, Sojourner was living in one of the temporary wood-frame buildings that housed ex-slaves fleeing north.

Even as Sojourner dictated the letter, she must have been thinking of the next task that lay ahead of her. For no one looking at Freedman's Village could escape the signs of dejection, degradation, and poverty that could be seen everywhere.

Children standing in breadlines looked up at Sojourner Truth with hungry eyes. Black women who had only worked in the fields asked her to teach them the basics of housekeeping. The sullen despair of jobless black men hung like a cloud over the teeming village.

In the eyes and the voices and the expressions of Sojourner's people, she could read a clear message. The slaves were free. Yes, they were free at last. But they had no place to go.

CHAPTER ELEVEN

Freedom Rider

Ku Klux Klan founded 1865

MURDER BAY

uring the Civil War, slaves who fled to the Union side were called "contraband of war." In Washington, D.C. and many other cities, "contraband" could not ride streetcars with whites. They were barred from living in all white neighborhoods. Even if they could have afforded it, they would not have been allowed to attend many schools. Most churches, as well, were segregated.

By 1864 when Sojourner arrived in the nation's capital, it was flooded with former slaves cast adrift when emancipation cut the ties of bondage. To many of them, Washington, D.C. was the city of hope. Wasn't this where the Great Emancipator, Abraham Lincoln, lived?

Along the Washington Canal, a hundred families crowded into an area half the size of today's football field.

Shacks had no windows or plumbing. They were filthy. Among the white citizens of Washington the area was called "Murder Bay."

Even Mr. Lincoln could not think of a way to meet the crisis that was overwhelming his city. He could not make enough room for all the blacks who had come north, nor could he feed all the hungry children who roamed the streets.

Freedman's Village, where Sojourner took up residence, was located across the Potomac River. Conditions in the temporary Village were certainly better than in Murder Bay. But many of the ex-slaves who lived in the long, wood-frame rowhouses were in desperate need of help.

Slavery left permanent scars. Up to the time the slaves were freed, all the organization and economy of their lives had been in the master's hands. Food, shelter, clothing—all the basic necessities had been provided by someone else. The master was even responsible for their children.

Emancipated slaves had the look of people stunned by misfortune, as indeed they were. One observer of the time described them this way:

> They had a dreamy look, taking no note of time; it seemed as if a pause had come in their lives—an abyss, over whose brink they dared not look. With so few resources, with no education from books or contact with the world aside from plantation life—strangers in a

strange land, hungry, thirsty, ragged, homeless—they were the very image of despair.

Living among the contraband of war, Sojourner realized how much had yet to be done. The emancipated slaves had to learn everything—*everything*! Managing households, looking for jobs, educating children, even asking for assistance—all the things that white people took for granted were new to the people who had just been born again in a different life.

The challenge was enormous. Yet the people Sojourner met were eager to learn. And when she spoke, they came to listen.

After some months in Freedman's Village, Sojourner approached Captain Carse, who was the chief administrator. Could she and Sammy stay on in the village and assist her people? "They have to learn to be free," she insisted.

On December 1, 1864 a letter arrived from New York:

This certifies that The National Freedman's Relief Association has appointed Sojourner Truth to be a counselor to the freed people at Arlington Heights, Virginia, and hereby commends her to the favor and confidence of the offices of government.

But Sojourner Truth had not been idle while waiting for the letter to arrive. She had discovered that terrible crimes against black people were being committed every day. She wasn't going to stand by and do nothing!

Slave traders were preying on the residents of Freedman's Village!

In the Confederate states, slaves were free. But not in Maryland. There, the state courts were still debating a law abolishing slavery.

To feed the Maryland slave trade, bands of cutthroat traders lurked on the outskirts of Freedman's Village. They struck suddenly, seized wailing children and dragged them away to sell in Maryland. The slave traders were defying the laws of Virginia. But Captain Carse, administrator of Freedman's Village, did nothing to stop them.

It was Sojourner Truth who put an end to the kidnapping.

She rallied soldiers who were strong antislavery men. The next time kidnappers descended on the village, Sojourner's soldiers were waiting for them with fixed bayonets. The soldiers pounced on the slave traders, surrounded them, and demanded that they release the children.

While soldiers held the kidnappers at bay, the frightened children rushed off to the arms of their mothers.

The slavers cursed the tall, white-bonneted black woman who shook her cane at them. "We'll have you thrown in the guardhouse, old lady," they threatened her.

"If you attempt it, children, I will make the United States rock like a cradle!" she retorted.

Sojourner's act of defiance lifted the cloud of dread from Freedman's Village. Antislavery soldiers remained on the alert, but the kidnappers had been sufficiently warned. They did not return. Now Sojourner could concentrate on the real task at hand. She had to teach these women the basics of cooking, cleaning, and caring for children.

They were eager to learn. But their needs were almost overwhelming. Each day, more ex-slaves arrived, until they almost burst from the boundaries of the small compound. The Freedman's Bureau was furnishing seven hundred loaves of bread a day, but even that was not enough to feed those already in the Village. And now babies were being born—more mouths to feed!

After nearly a year's work at Freedman's Village, Sojourner was appointed to work in Freedman's Hospital. In the letter of recommendation, the assistant commissioner noted her "energetic and faithful efforts." Her future responsibilities, as he described them, were to "aid in promoting order, cleanliness, industry, and virtue among the patients."

In her work for the hospital, Sojourner had to travel to many areas of D.C. and Georgetown. Horsedrawn streetcars clacked along rails through the city streets. Sojourner was told that she could only ride the "Jim Crow" car set aside for blacks. She refused. In protest, she walked where she wanted to go, often carrying large bundles in her arms.

Not for long!

After a few days of this, Sojourner Truth went directly to the president of the street railroad to register an official complaint. When the deep-voiced, six-foot-tall, grandmotherly black woman strode into his office, the president paid attention. Sojourner set down her pipe, put aside her cane, and began lecturing him on the principles of equality.

This was the woman who had met with Abraham Lincoln. What could he do but listen?

Sojourner had her way. The Jim Crow car was immediately taken out of service. Soon after, a law was passed giving black people the right to ride the streetcars with whites.

However, as Sojourner had discovered many times before, there was a huge gap between the law in theory and the law in practice. Streetcar conductors and drivers were not easily changed in their ways. They ignored the new rules. Just as before, black people were passed by when they tried to hail streetcars.

But they couldn't ignore Sojourner.

The next time a streetcar driver tried to ignore her, she dashed after the car.

"I want to ride!" she shouted.

When the car did not slow down, she raised her voice even louder and waved her cane.

"*I want to ride!!* I WANT TO RIDE!!!"

All traffic on the street came to a halt. People crowded around to see what was happening. The car was forced to stop. Before it could move on, Sojourner made a flying leap, grabbed the handrail, and flung herself, breathless, among the startled white passengers.

By now, the crowd was cheering her on. "She has beaten him!" they laughed.

The streetcar conductor approached her menacingly. "Go forward where the horses are, or I will throw you out," he commanded.

"I know the laws as well as you do," she replied. "This is my seat and I will stay here."

And she did, riding the car farther than she needed to go. In fact, she rode all the way to the end of the line.

"Bless God! I have had a ride!" she said as she got off.

But the battle was not won. Again and again, conductors would try to ignore her or throw her off. Indignant white passengers would stand up and demand, "Conductor, conductor—do niggers ride these cars?"

Sojourner knew her rights and refused to budge.

The controversy continued until one day when Sojourner was riding back from the hospital with Laura Haviland, a famous philanthropist. Mrs. Haviland was well aware that a white person was not allowed to ride if accompanied by a black. But she chose to ignore the unwritten rule. She waved to a passing streetcar so she and Sojourner could climb aboard.

Some months later, Sojourner told her friends the story of what happened next:

When the streetcar stopped, I ran and jumped aboard. The conductor pushed me back, saying, "Get out of the way and let this lady come in."

"Whoop!" said I, "I am a lady too!"

We met with no further opposition until we were obliged to change cars. Then, a man coming out as we were going into the next car asked the conductor if "niggers were allowed to ride."

The conductor grabbed me by the shoulder, jerked me around and ordered me to get out.

I told him I would not.

Mrs. Haviland took hold of my other arm and said, "Don't put her out."

The conductor asked if I belonged to her.

"No," replied Mrs. Haviland, "she belongs to humanity!"

"Then take her and go," said the conductor. And giving me another push, he slammed me against the door.

I told him I would let him know whether he could shove me about like a dog.

"Take the number of this car," I said to Mrs. Haviland.

The conductor knew he would be in trouble if a white woman filed a complaint. He made no more trouble during the trip.

But Sojourner was not done. When she arrived at the hospital, she called a surgeon to examine her shoulder. He confirmed what she suspected. The shoulder had been dislocated when the conductor slammed her against the door.

After the arm had been treated, Sojourner returned

113

to the president of the street railroad, the man she had met before. He listened to her story with growing anger.

"I take no responsibility for that man's action," he said finally. "Have him arrested for assault and battery—and I'll see that he's fired. That's all I can promise you."

Sojourner promptly went to the Freedman's Bureau, which furnished her a lawyer. The conductor was brought to trial. Sojourner elaborated the exact details of the incident.

The court found the conductor guilty of assault and battery, and the next day he was fired.

Within a few weeks, Sojourner Truth had completely integrated the streetcar system in Washington, D.C.

"Before the trial was ended," she declared, "the insides of the cars looked like pepper and salt."

CHAPTER TWELVE

Land of the Free

Charles Sumner

COTTON FIELDS

Integrating the streetcars of Washington was a significant achievement.

But as Sojourner saw it, a former slave had a right to far more than a seat on a streetcar. Black men and women had served their white masters for decades. Their contributions in skill and labor translated into millions of dollars of profit for Southern plantations and Northern mills. But no slave had ever been compensated. Sojourner's thoughts on this subject came together eloquently in one of her speeches:

We have been a source of wealth to this republic. Our labor supplied the country with cotton, until villages and cities dotted the enterprising North for its manufac-

115

ture—and furnished employment and support for a multitude, thereby becoming a revenue to the government. Beneath a burning Southern sun have we toiled, in the canebrake and the rice swamp, urged on by the merciless driver's lash, earning millions of money.

Our nerves and sinews, our tears and blood, have been sacrificed on the altar of this nation's avarice. Our unpaid labor has been a steppingstone to its financial success. Some of its dividends must surely be ours.

It was too late, now, to pay back the slaves for all those hours of labor. And no payment could ever be made for the human loss, grief and suffering. But the United States did have one source of great richness that it could bequeath to the freed slaves. It had land!

As Sojourner Truth looked around her at the blacks crowded into Freedman's Village, she saw that her people needed precisely what America could easily give them.

They needed land!

Land where crops could be sown and harvested. Land where children could be raised. Land for houses, for schools, for churches, and for public meeting places. Land untainted by a history of slave and master.

Every immigrant to America had sought one thing first—property! Once a person owned property, everything else became possible. But Africans had come chained in the holds of ships, and they remained the property of others.

Now was their first chance to become the owners

instead of the owned. Sojourner Truth asked for nothing more for her people—just a chance!

As Sojourner began to form her new plan, she thought of how she would present it to the one man who would understand, Abraham Lincoln. But on the night of April 14, 1865, all hope of seeing Lincoln again ended in the shot from a hand-held derringer.

Attending a play at Ford's Theater, Abraham Lincoln was shot by the actor John Wilkes Booth.

He died early the next morning.

His death was a deep personal grief to Sojourner. But as time passed, she realized that she must persist without Lincoln. Surely there were men in Congress who would be sympathetic to her cause. Somehow, she must get them to listen to her great scheme.

As she talked to friends about her plan, she realized that there might be a way. If she could draw up a petition directed toward Congress, the mighty senators would *have* to listen to her!

The first draft of her petition was dictated to Sammy. It was addressed "TO THE SENATE AND HOUSE OF REPRESENTATIVES, in Congress assembled":

> From the faithful and earnest representations of Sojourner Truth (who has personally investigated the matter), we believe that the freed colored people in and about Washington, dependent upon government for support, would be greatly benefited and might become useful citizens by being placed in a position to support themselves:

We, the undersigned, therefore request you to set apart for them a portion of the public land in the West.

Sojourner gathered a number of signatures in favor of the petition. Then she prepared to argue her case.

She could point out that large land grants had been made to the railroads. Millions of acres had been donated free to the railroad barons so they could lay down rails and run trains for profit! Why couldn't some measure of land be given to blacks as well?

Also, there was a precedent for the kind of land grant that she was proposing. Hadn't the United States government given reservations to the Indians? Why not reserve similar tracts of land for freed slaves? The people in Freedman's Village, she insisted, "would rather become independent through their own exertions than clog the wheels of government."

After the Civil War, blacks needed their own territory where they could rebuild their lives again, without prejudice or fear. But who would listen to such a radical idea?

Sojourner was determined that people *would* listen. Her campaign would begin right here, in Washington, D.C. First the White House—then, Capitol Hill!

On March 31, 1870 she called on the new president of the United States, Ulysses S. Grant. Before she told him about her plan, she wanted to offer her personal thanks for an event that had taken place the day before. On the 30th of March, Congress had ratified the Sixteenth

Amendment, giving all Americans, regardless of color, the right to vote.

Grant signed Sojourner's "Book of Life." Though we do not know exactly the content of their conversation, it is unlikely that he supported her idea of a land grant to black people. His words to her on that subject were probably not encouraging.

A month later, an historic event took place. On April 26, 1870, seventy-three-year-old Sojourner Truth visited the halls and chambers of the Capitol building. All government business came to a halt for a few minutes at the amazing vision of the tall, white-capped woman in gray, rustling skirts who strode through the corridors on her way to see the senators.

In the following week's Sunday paper, a reporter tried to convey the electric excitement that accompanied her steps:

> It was an hour not soon to be forgotten. It was refreshing, but also strange, to see a woman born in the shackles of slavery now treated to a reception by senators in a marble room. A decade ago she would have been spurned from its outer corridor by the lowest menial. . . . Truly, the spirit of progress is abroad in the land!

While fourteen senators clustered around to sign her book, the others looked on benevolently, talking among themselves. Many regarded Sojourner Truth as a novelty—an "original" who had survived with dignity all the changes of the past decade. But few of those congressmen supported the ambitious scheme she proposed on behalf of her people.

The final senator to approach her was the exception. He was as tall as she, with bleach-white hair and a lined, serious face. She recognized him immediately—Charles Sumner, the senator from Massachusetts, who had cursed the fugitive slave laws, denounced the Kansas-Nebraska Act, and launched devastating verbal attacks on Southern slaveholders.

In 1856, senators in that marble chamber had stood by while a proslavery man attacked Sumner with a stick and beat him over the head. It was three years before the senator completely recovered.

Sumner invited Sojourner to his office where they could speak privately. There he signed her book and listened to her plea.

He was sobered by her ambitious plan. More than all the other men in Congress, he knew what a long, hard fight lay ahead of her. Gazing at the sturdy old woman, he must have wondered whether she had the strength to persevere.

But she talked as if nothing could stop her. So Sumner took the first step. He advised her to get more signatures on her petition—thousands, even tens of thousands. If this wild plan of hers had the ghost of a chance, it would need the weight of many endorsements behind it.

When she returned with those names, he would see what could be done.

In her book he wrote, "Equality of rights is the first

of rights. Charles Sumner, Senate Chamber, April 26, 1870."

In the five long years ahead, there were many times when Sojourner would turn to that signature in her "Book of Life" and draw strength from it.

For the great plan she had in mind, it was the one ray of hope that shone through all the days to come.

Squaring her shoulders and tucking the "Book of Life" under her arm, Sojourner called Sammy to her side and headed north to collect the signatures she needed. In February 1870 she delivered her first lecture in Providence, Rhode Island.

Soon, reports flooded in from newspapers throughout the Northeast:

"The renowned Sojourner Truth spoke in the town hall last evening . . ." began an article in the Northampton, Massachusetts *Journal*. "Petitions have been placed in the hands of friends of this movement, and it is hoped that every person will sign."

"Sojourner Truth will speak at the vestry of the First M.E. Church tomorrow evening . . ." announced the papers in Fall River, Massachusetts. "Enjoy a half hour with a ripe understanding, and don't forget to purchase her photograph."

"Springfield, Union County, New Jersey, and its Presbyterian Church were honored on Wednesday night by the presence of Sojourner Truth, who years ago was wont to address street meetings and Garrison abolition conventicles . . ."

Throughout Rhode Island, Massachusetts, Connecticut, New Jersey, New York—then back to Massachusetts—Sojourner and Sammy traveled from town to town. Scores of names soon added up to hundreds, hundreds to thousands as she tirelessly explained her urgent mission. Soon the single page of the petition was backed by many pages of signatures, all tied together with yellow string.

It was this tour that brought her to Tremont Hall in Boston on January 1, 1871—the eighth anniversary of the Emancipation Proclamation.

There, once again, she preceded her plea for signatures by first telling the story of her life.

CHAPTER THIRTEEN

No Hearing for Her Cause

President Ulysses S. Grant

THE CAPITOL

The story of a little girl named Isabella and her flight toward freedom had a profound impact on the Bostonians in Tremont Hall. By the time Sojourner Truth had finished, the audience was captivated. Everything they had heard about her was true!

Harriet Beecher Stowe, in her *Atlantic* article, had written, "I never knew a person who possessed so much of that subtle, controlling personal power as she."

Now the Boston audience understood what Mrs. Stowe had meant. By the time Sojourner Truth finished the story of her life, everyone was under the spell of "that subtle, controlling personal power."

123

But Sojourner did not waste that power on self-glorification. She was pursuing a cause that was far more important than personal glory. She had met with these Boston churchgoers not to impress them but to draw them to her cause. And she needed their signatures!

Toward the end of the speech, her voice took on new depth and richness as her words turned to a simple plea. There was an uncomfortable stir in the audience. One gentleman glanced at another, pulled at his tight collar and sniffed. There was a rustle of starched dresses.

All had read the newspaper reports. They knew this woman would not let them be complacent. She had once described herself as the flea who kept biting. People might not like what she said, but she would make them scratch!

Now, Sojourner Truth turned her penetrating gaze on the audience:

Here is the question that I have come to ask tonight. I have been to Washington and I have found out that the black people in Washington are living on the government. That is costing you so much—and it doesn't benefit the black man at all. It degrades him worse and worse.

Therefore I say, give the emancipated people land and move them on it. Put them in the West where you can enrich them. I know the good people in the South can't take care of the Negroes as they ought to, because the rebels won't let them. How much better it would be if you could take those black people and give them land. It would be a benefit for all of you, and God would bless all of you for doing it.

Now some people say, "Let the blacks take care of themselves." But you've taken everything away from them. They don't have anything left!

I say, get the black people out of Washington! Get them off the government! Get the old people out and build them homes in the West, where they can feed themselves. Lift up those people and put them there. Teach them to read part of the time and teach them to work the other part of the time. Do that, and they will soon be a *people* among you.

That is my commission!

The tension in the audience now broke. A portly gentleman in a gray frock coat got to his feet, banging his cane rudely on the floor. His face was beet red.

Give land to the colored? What an idea! This black woman must be mad!

Strutting past the pews, he shook his head and muttered to himself. A wave of whispers flooded the audience. People glanced up at the platform to see what Sojourner would do next.

Would there now be a mass exodus from the hall?

A deep voice rolled from the front of the sanctuary.

"I'll hold on a while," said Sojourner. The murmurs subsided. "Whoever is going, let him go." She paused, her gaze sweeping the audience.

"When you talk about *work* around here," Sojourner continued easily, "then people begin to *scoot*!"

The audience burst into applause and laughter. So-

UNCLE TOM'S CABIN

journer's serious face broke into a smile. "I tell you, I can't read a book, but I can read the people."

Again there was applause.

She took a step toward them and the crowd was stilled again. Her crippled hand, injured long before in Master Dumont's field, was tucked under the fringe of her plain white shawl. Her small spectacles glinted white with the reflection of the gas lamps that lined the walls of the hall. Far away, outside the double doors of the temple, there was a rattle of wheels on cobblestone and crack of a whip as the indignant gentleman rode away in his carriage.

"I speak these things," pronounced Sojourner in a low, steady voice, "so that when a paper comes around for you to sign, you can *sign* it."

Without another word, she returned to her chair, sat down and folded her hands in her lap. But Sammy was already moving among the pews, distributing his grand-mother's petition.

Thunderous applause shook the rafters of Tremont Hall.

Eight years before, a tall, gaunt president battered by the daily tragedies of war had signed the Emancipation Proclamation. Now, nearly a decade later, that spirit was reborn in the form of a seventy-four-year-old black woman with a powerful voice and high ideals.

On the eighth anniversary of the historical signing, the Bostonians in Tremont Hall readily applied their pens to the petition of Sojourner Truth.

As Sojourner continued on her journey to gather sig-natures, her life assumed a steady pattern. She was driven by the necessity to complete the task that lay before her.

She and Sammy would rise at the crack of dawn to take a carriage to the next meeting place. For long hours, she gave speeches, answered hecklers, discussed, pleaded, argued. Never staying long in one place, she relied on friends, acquaintances, and sympathizers to help her on her way.

She never lost hope.

There must have been many times when she thought of her comfortable house and garden in Battle Creek. The Merritts had taken good care of it for her. A government pension, partial payment for her work for the Freedman's

Bureau, was paying off the small mortgage. She could easily retire at any time.

But whenever she thought of that welcoming, familiar home with its broad lawn and sunny garden, she would glance at the pile of petitions weighing down her carpetbag. Her eyes fed on the rows and rows of signatures, names that she could not even read. She gathered strength from the numbers.

She had changed the minds of all these people. She had planted a seed. If she stopped her work, her great plan would die on the vine. She alone could achieve success in this mission. It was up to Sojourner Truth to win land for her people.

With these thoughts in her mind, she called Sammy to her side every evening. "Where is our next engagement?" she would ask him. He would leaf through the letters and invitations that poured in from Sojourner's friends and admirers. Glancing at the engagement book that he kept for his grandmother, he would name their next destination.

Sojourner's worn face lit up when Sammy mentioned the names of her old friends from the antislavery and women's rights movements. She could hardly wait to see them again.

"Let us rise early," she would tell Sammy. "We need to get a good start on the day."

As she traveled, Sojourner also had to consider what lay at the end of the road. Back in Washington, she would have to present the tens of thousands of signatures she had collected. So much depended on Charles Sumner. Would he be able to rally the congressional support she needed?

Sumner would not be halfhearted about any cause he embraced. She knew that. He would declare with all the force of conviction, "We enslaved these people for two hundred years. They have earned this land—and now we must give it to them!"

Who, besides Sumner, could understand the pressing need of all black people to have land of their own?

Across all those miles, Charles Sumner was the light of hope that beckoned her onward.

But now she wondered. Would he still be there, prepared to help her when she most needed him?

By 1873 Sojourner and Sammy had carried their stack of petitions, wrapped in yellow string, from the eastern states to the Midwest. After stopping for awhile with Amy and Isaac Post in Rochester, they pushed on through Ohio toward Kansas.

Sojourner had a double reason for wanting to reach Kansas. More signatures were to be found there, certainly. But also, this was the very land she was fighting to win. From her previous visit she had recalled the acres of rich soil and the yellowish, waving wheat on the plots that were planted. Seeing it all again, even more prosperous than before, reminded her of the promise that this land held for her people.

Her speeches had a renewed fervor. Throughout the fall and winter, she traveled from Topeka to Lawrence,

Wyandotte, and Leavenworth. By February 1874, she and Sammy were in Iowa. They passed through Illinois in April, Missouri in July.

In August she was back in Battle Creek, where she wanted to campaign and vote for Ulysses Grant, the president she had met in person. He had not offered much hope, but at least she had met him. Now she wanted to keep him in office until she could return to Washington.

But Sojourner Truth was not permitted to vote!

When she went to register, she was asked, "Can you read and write?"

She had to say no. The registrar shrugged his shoulders. "Then you can't vote," he told Sojourner.

Throughout the North and South, this scene was being repeated everywhere, in thousands of voting places. Blacks who tried to register were denied their rights. What was happening at each polling place made a mockery of the Sixteenth Amendment. The "right to vote" had been granted in theory. But in practice, it was still beyond reach.

Enraged, Sojourner stalked into the Battle Creek newspaper office and told the editor what she intended to do.

"It is Sojourner's determination," the editor commented dryly in his column, "to continue the assertion of her right to vote until she gains it."

But a greater urgency drew her away from Battle Creek.

There was bad news about the United States Congress. Alarmed by the number of blacks now in Washington—nearly one quarter of the capital's population—Sumner's fellow politicians passed a bill that specifically denied Negroes the right to vote in the District of Columbia.

Sumner demanded that the bill be withdrawn. But despite his eloquence, the act was passed. In the nation's capital, blacks were once again disenfranchised.

Every day, it seemed, blacks were beginning to lose ground they had gained. Worst of all, now there was creeping indifference to the entire issue. The War was over. In the North and South, white people were trying to get on with business. The problems of ex-slaves were too complicated and overwhelming for the nation's voters. Everyone was trying to forget.

In early 1874 Sojourner set out with Sammy for Washington, D.C. The pile of petitions was never out of their sight. As usual, Sojourner took advantage of every opportunity to meet with people, to speak and solicit signatures. She was particularly interested in meeting political leaders who might help her cause.

Sojourner sat in the jolting coach on the last leg of her journey, the weighty sheaf of petitions clutched tightly in her hands. The time had come. She must go to Charles Sumner and place the petitions on his desk. She would argue her case, but the decision would be left in his hands. He was her greatest hope.

Once again, Sojourner and Sammy strode down the marble congressional corridor where they had first set foot four years before. When they came to the door of the great senator's office, Sammy knocked.

After a long delay, a congressional page answered.

When Sammy announced what they had come for, the page shook his head.

No, he was very sorry, Senator Charles Sumner would be unable to see them.

On March 10 the senator had suffered a heart attack while speaking in Congress. The page regretted to inform them that the senator had died the same day.

The page explained that he was just answering the final correspondence before closing up Senator Sumner's office for the last time.

CHAPTER FOURTEEN

The Power of Conviction

SHOOTING STAR

S ojourner Truth was a fighter.

She had faced discouragement many times in her life. When white people told her she couldn't have her son back, when they told her she could not attend their services or ride their streetcars, when they told her she could not vote—she had spoken out to get what she wanted.

Although she was now seventy-seven years old, her character had not changed. If Charles Sumner was no longer alive to fight for the land bill, she would do it herself in her own way. She had lost one powerful friend

133

and she faced many powerful enemies. But she would not give up the cause she had pursued during four long years.

She and Sammy stayed in Washington. As spring gave way to the sweltering, cloying Washington summer, the heat drained their energy but not their determination. Day after day, Sojourner carried the parcel tied in yellow string from door to door, rephrasing her plea.

When a congressman agreed to meet with her, she thought there might yet be hope.

Then, one midsummer morning, the last glimmer of hope faded.

That morning, Sammy could not get up from his bed.

When his grandmother came in to see him, he was trembling and sweating. His eyes were wide with fear. He had the gray look of one who was dying.

As the sun rose higher in the sky and the heat burned through the still, humid air of the city, Sammy shook violently, as if his whole body were freezing.

"Sammy—God help you, Sammy!" Sojourner clutched his chill, trembling hand. "We will go home."

She hardly even glanced at the bundle of petitions that she dropped in her carpetbag. Hastily, she stuffed their few clothes into bags and crates. She stopped every few minutes, whenever Sammy cried out, to bring him water or press a damp cloth to his head.

Leaving behind the gleaming dome of the nation's Capitol, Sojourner set off without a backward glance. Her destination was home—home to the cool, tree-

CARPET BAG

shaded Michigan town where the gentle summer breezes would restore her grandson's health again.

Sammy survived the trip, but his health continued to decline rapidly. No one knew what was wrong with him. Sojourner blamed the heat and dust of Washington, because she knew the toll it had taken on both of them.

Yet being in Battle Creek did not bring about the recovery she expected. Every day, Sammy was a little bit worse. Sojourner nursed him, but that winter she herself suffered a minor stroke. She was partially paralyzed on one side of her body. She also developed painful ulcers on her legs that made it difficult and sometimes impossible for her to move.

In February of 1875, Sammy died. He was close to twenty-five years old.

The grandson who had been at her side for years was gone.

135

Sojourner believed that she soon would follow him.

But Sojourner Truth would outlive her grandson by nearly nine years.

As crocuses pushed their way up through the melting snow, Sojourner Truth began to recover. Among the first to visit her was Frances Titus, a good friend who frequently wrote for newspapers and journals. Mrs. Titus had urged Sojourner to update the 1850 edition of the *Narrative*. To the original *Narrative* Mrs. Titus wanted to add articles, selections from Sojourner's speeches, and names from the "Book of Life."

That spring, as Mrs. Titus sat with her outside the Merritts' house, Sojourner finally agreed. Mrs. Titus immediately began writing a new entry to go in the book. It was a message to all of Sojourner's followers as well as her new readers:

Sojourner suffered from serious illness during the winter, and her life was despaired of for many long weeks. But her friends now rejoice to see her convalescing. She feels that for some special purpose her life has been spared, comparative health restored, and her mind brought back from the shadowy realm where it wandered during the days and nights when that red-lipped demon, Fever, with insatiate thirst, sucked the juices from life's fountain. She says, "My good Master kept me, for he had something for me to do."

Mrs. Titus soon completed the updated edition of

the *Narrative.* Its republication served a practical purpose. Once again, Sojourner had a book to sell. When she had no other means of income, sale of the book could help support her.

Seeing her book in print also provided a new incentive to travel. Sojourner would soon be on the road again.

Beginning in December, 1877, astonishing reports began to reach Sojourner at the little house in Battle Creek. A migration had begun. Freed slaves, leaving the South, were heading north toward Kansas.

To Sojourner this was a signal that her dream might come true. If blacks were claiming the land for themselves, no congressional act was necessary. Perhaps the need for a land grant had outlived its hour.

Sojourner began to take renewed interest in speaking and politics. Soon after her eightieth birthday, she appeared at a number of meetings, testifying for women's rights, prison reform, temperance, and the rights of working men. When she was invited to speak about capital punishment before the Michigan State senate, she appeared in a bright red shawl.

"The person who wants to see his fellow beings hung by the neck until dead has a murderous spot in his heart," she proclaimed to the senators.

In 1878 she traveled on a speaking tour to thirty-six different towns in Michigan. In July of that year, the eighty-one-year-old woman was one of three Michigan delegates to the Women's Rights Convention in Rochester.

Turning her eyes West, Sojourner looked toward

Kansas. It was a long distance to travel, but she could not stay away. By 1879 she had heard that sixty thousand blacks had made the grueling trip from such faraway places as Concordia, Louisiana; Yazoo, Mississippi; Mobile, Alabama; and Little Rock, Arkansas.

Yet there was disturbing news as well. A great number of the new arrivals were moving into cities, where they would only find jobs as day laborers at poor wages. Many of them, she knew, would find no jobs at all! The newspapers were publishing pictures of black men, women, and children crammed into public buildings.

To Sojourner these pictures were a grim reminder of Freedman's Village!

Sojourner knew there was no room for blacks in the cities. They had to go to the country, where there was land for them—land they could own! They should take advantage of the Homestead Law. Did they realize they could lay claim to land, simply by applying to the public land office? Homesteaders could farm one hundred sixty acres of public land for five years without paying a dime for it. Surely that was a chance to get started!

If black people didn't know about these land opportunities, they would soon find out. Sojourner Truth was going to tell them!

Late in 1879 she packed a box of "Shadows" and the new edition of her *Narrative* into a wagon and headed south toward Topeka. The governor of Kansas had made a speech at the Topeka Opera House, welcoming freed slaves to his state. The Freedman's Relief Association had been set up in May. Many friends from antislavery days and leaders of the women's rights struggle were headed in the same direction.

Sojourner would meet them in Kansas!

It was her last, long journey.

When she returned to Battle Creek, she was ready to rest. Though she had completely recovered from her earlier stroke, the ulcers on her legs still bothered her. An extraordinary physician, Dr. John Harvey Kellogg, director of the Battle Creek Sanitarium, examined her with great care. He recommended skin grafts, a completely new procedure in those days. But when he asked for donors, he could not get any volunteers.

Dr. Kellogg did not hesitate. He took grafts from his own skin. The grafts were successful. But when later outbreaks were more severe, Dr. Kellogg was unable to do anything more for Sojourner.

In the fall of 1883 Sojourner Truth was near death. Frances Titus, the woman who had updated the *Narrative*, was a constant companion at her bedside. A journalist who visited the house described what he saw:

> In a half reclining position on a bed, her back bolstered up with pillows, lay Sojourner Truth. She said nothing until made aware of Mrs. Titus's presence, when she lifted her head slightly, displaying a great wrinkled and emaciated face. Her eyes were bright as they have ever been. Her illness is very severe and causes her great pain. All hope is now given up of a restoration to health.

A few days later, in a moment of clarity, Sojourner looked up at a friend and declared serenely, "I'm not going to die, honey. I'm going home like a shooting star."

Sojourner Truth died at 3 A.M. on the morning of November 26, 1883.

"This country has lost one of its most remarkable personages," said a Battle Creek newspaper.

More than a thousand people listened to a sermon delivered by Sojourner's friend, the Reverend Reed Stuart, then followed her casket to the Oakhill Cemetery. Tributes and testimonials appeared in newspapers around the country.

Sitting at the desk where he had edited so many issues of *The North Star*, Frederick Douglass recalled the tall, determined woman who, like he, had been born into slavery. They had walked parallel roads, but parted on many issues. He recalled vividly the clear, deep voice that had rolled over the heads of the audience, issuing a challenge that would haunt him for years afterward. When he had called for bloodshed and retribution, she had demanded:

"Frederick, is God dead?"

That was a question he still could not answer.

He glanced up at the bookshelf. There, alongside his own life story was her own slim volume, the *Narrative of Sojourner Truth*. Before him on the desk was a single song sheet with one of her hymns, and a brown-tinted portrait with the inscription, "The Shadow supports the Substance."

With these reminders surrounding him, the black man penned the first words of his tribute: "She was a woman venerable for age, distinguished for insight into human nature, remarkable for independence and courageous self-assertion. . . ."

If you visit Battle Creek today, you will find Sojourner Truth's tall marble gravestone flanked by boxwood hedges. Alongside is an historical marker honoring her children and grandchildren who are buried nearby.

Stand in front of that peaceful monument and you may find it hard to imagine how she stirred thousands of people during her lifetime. We have no recordings of that great, rolling voice—and of course no one can duplicate the power of her presence. Sojourner spoke from the heart, and each word carried the force of her personal wisdom and experience.

But we can recognize her challenge.

Again and again, Sojourner Truth challenged people to exercise their greatest freedom, the right to speak. She could not release her people from the bondage of slavery or poverty. She could not overturn the laws of the country. She could not get her land grant bill passed by Congress.

But she could *speak*! And her ringing tones can still be heard today:

"I want to tell you these things that you will always remember. And I say this to you all—for a great many people are here—that when I step out of this existence, you will know what you heard old Sojourner Truth tell you!"

Abolitionism

A movement with religious roots, abolitionism opposed slavery on moral grounds and worked to put an end to it.

American Anti-Slavery Society

Society founded by William Lloyd Garrison and other leading abolitionists to oppose slavery. The Society organized meetings, brought in speakers, published pamphlets, and generally tried to make the cause of abolitionism known and understood.

Confederacy

When the Southern states wanted to separate from the United States, this is what they called themselves. The soldiers who fought for the South were called "Confederates."

Cravat

A band or scarf worn around the neck.

Douglass, Frederick

An escaped slave who became one of the strongest and most effective speakers against slavery. A noted writer and intellectual, Douglass was the publisher of *The North Star*, the leading black newspaper of the time, and author of the *Narrative of the Life of Frederick Douglass*.

Dred Scott Case

Dred Scott was a slave who lived a number of years

in Missouri. Upon his master's death he sued for his freedom on the grounds that he had lived in an area where slavery was outlawed by the Missouri Compromise. The court's decision, made in 1857, denied Scott his freedom in terms that effectively declared the Missouri Compromise unconstitutional and gave blacks no basic rights under the Constitution.

Emancipation Proclamation

This was the document, signed by President Abraham Lincoln on January 1, 1863, that ended slavery forever in the United States. It reads, in part, "All persons held as slaves in any state . . . shall be henceforward and forever free."

First National Women's Rights Convention

Women from across the nation met in 1851 at Worcester, Massachusetts to discuss women's rights, including the right to vote.

Freedman's Villages

Temporary settlements where former slaves lived after the Civil War.

Freedom Rider

A term for blacks who protested the enforced segregation on public transportation by riding on "whites only" trains and buses, and sitting in seats reserved for whites. Sojourner Truth was the first Freedom Rider, but in the 1960's, almost a hundred years later, Freedom Riders were to become an important part of the black civil rights struggle. Rosa Parks became the most famous modern Freedom Rider when she refused to give up her seat on a bus to a white person in Montgomery, Alabama.

Fugitive Slave Law

Passed in 1850, the Fugitive Slave Law required that the full authority of the federal government be placed at the service of slave owners seeking to get back runaway slaves. The law essentially denied all slaves any of the basic rights guaranteed under the Constitution, including the right to a jury trial and testifying on their own behalf.

Garrison, William Lloyd

A leader of the Abolitionist Movement, Garrison was a fiery speaker and a man of strong principles. Fervently opposed to slavery, he was also a strong supporter of women's rights.

Grant, Ulysses S.

Union Army general during the Civil War, later to become president

Hooker, Joseph

Union Army general during the Civil War.

Jim Crow

A group of laws passed after the Civil War to enforce segregation, or separation of blacks and whites. Jim Crow laws enforced such restrictions as separate black and white train cars, lunch counters, restrooms, drinking fountains, and so on.

Kansas–Nebraska Act

Passed in 1854, this Act allowed the slavery issue to be decided on the basis of popular vote in the newly opened Kansas-Nebraska territory. It explicitly re-

pealed the Missouri Compromise of 1850 which pro-
hibited slavery in all territories of the United States
north of Missouri's southern border.

Lee, Robert E.

The general in command of the Confederate Army.

The Liberator

Abolitionist newspaper founded in Boston in 1831 by
William Lloyd Garrison. *The Liberator* soon became the
major antislavery voice in the country.

Low Dutch

Form of Dutch spoken by certain Dutch immigrants
to America, particularly in New York and
Pennsylvania.

Mott, Lucretia

A leading abolitionist, feminist, and member of the
American Anti-Slavery Society.

Muckraking

This was the name given to investigative journalism in
the 1800's. Reporters searched out cases of misconduct
by prominent individuals.

Pinkster

A Dutch festival lasting seven days, falling seven weeks
after Easter.

Quakers

A Protestant religion that emphasizes good, simple liv-
ing. The Quakers, who are also called the Religious
Society of Friends, are opposed to war and slavery.
They often helped runaway slaves.

Sixteenth Amendment

Gave all Americans the right to vote regardless of race.

Slave Auction

The market where slaves were sold to the highest bidder.

Stowe, Harriet Beecher

A leading abolitionist and author of *Uncle Tom's Cabin*. Published in 1852, this was the most popular anti-slavery novel of its time.

Temperance Movement

A movement with its roots in the religious awakening of the 1830's which tried to encourage abstinence from alcohol.

Underground Railway

Organized by a group of escaped and freed slaves, most notably Harriet Tubman, the underground railway helped hundreds of slaves escape through a secret network of safe houses, often leading fugitive slaves all the way to Canada where they were beyond the reach of the Fugitive Slave Act.

York Shilling

A form of money used in New York during the early 1800's.

1. From your reading of the book, what did it mean to be a slave?
2. Sojourner Truth was the first Freedom Rider. What did this mean?
3. What did the Emancipation Proclamation say?
4. What was a Freedman's Village? What were they like?
5. Sojourner Truth said the Constitution of the United States had a "weevil" in it. What was she talking about?
6. Research Jim Crow laws. What were they? What were they designed to do? Why?
7. William Lloyd Garrison was one of the major leaders of the abolitionists. Describe some of the things he did. What did he hope abolitionism would accomplish?
8. Research the issues of the Dred Scott Case. What did the Dred Scott decision mean for black people in America?
9. What rights were women asking for that they did not have in America during Sojourner Truth's time?
10. Sojourner Truth said, "Our nerves and sinews, our tears and blood have been sacrificed on the altar of this nation's avarice. Our unpaid labor has been a stepping-stone to its financial success. Some of its dividends must surely be ours." What did she mean by this?

11. The South depended on slavery to a much greater degree than the North. Explain why this was so. Why do you feel that many Southerners refused to recognize that slavery was wrong?

12. Research the Fugitive Slave Law of 1850. How did it make worse the conflict between North and South?

13. Research the Kansas-Nebraska Act. How did it change the balance of slave and free states? Why did this threaten the union?

14. Present arguments for and against Sojourner Truth's Land Grant Plan. Do you agree or disagree with Sojourner Truth's plan?

15. Research abolitionism. Do you think the abolitionists were successful in their goals? How much do you think they helped bring about an end to slavery?

16. Frederick Douglass and Sojourner Truth disagreed about how to end slavery. What was the nature of their disagreement? Who do you think was right, if either?

17. The Northampton Association was a utopian community and many such communities existed in America at the time. What did this mean? What would be your idea of a utopia?

Tracing the Routes of Sojourner Truth

Sojourner Truth was deeply committed to the abolition of slavery in the United States. She made many long and dangerous journeys to bring attention to her cause. During the 1840's, she traveled all around New England talking to people she met at meetings and along the road.

Many years later, when the Civil War began, Sojourner Truth undertook another long journey from Michigan to Washington, D.C., in order to see the president. The route she took may be traced on the map on the facing page. Starting at Battle Creek, Michigan, she traveled to Detroit, and from Detroit to Chicago. Her next stop was Akron, Ohio. From there, she went to Rochester, New York, and then to New York City. From New York City, she went to Washington, D.C., and met with President Abraham Lincoln.

150

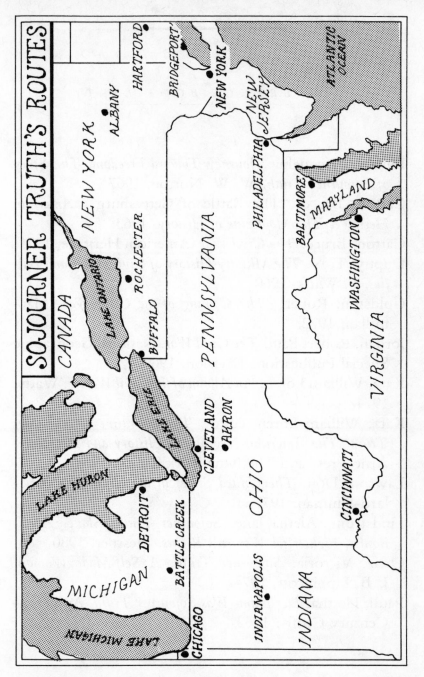

SOJOURNER TRUTH'S ROUTES

Bernard, Jacqueline. *Journey Toward Freedom: The Story of Sojourner Truth.* W. W. Norton, 1967.

Catton, Bruce. "The Battle of Gettysburg." *American Heritage, The Magazine of History*, 1963.

Catton, Bruce. *The Civil War.* American Heritage, 1971.

Dupuy, T. N. *The Military History of Civil War Land Battles.* F. Watts, 1960.

Goldston, Robert. *The Coming of the Civil War.* Macmillan, 1972.

Jordan, Robert Paul. *The Civil War.* National Geographic Special Publications Division, 1969.

Katz, William Loren. *An Album of the Civil War.* F. Watts, 1974.

Katz, William Loren, editor. *The Narrative of Sojourner Truth. The American Negro: His History and Literature.* Arno Press and The New York Times, 1968.

Lawson, Don. *The United States in the Civil War.* Abelard-Shuman, 1977.

Lindstrom, Aletha Jane. *Sojourner Truth: Slave, Abolitionist, Fighter for Women's Rights.* Messner, 1980.

Ortiz, Victoria. *Sojourner Truth, A Self-Made Woman.* J. B. Lippincott, 1974.

Pauli, Hertha. *Her Name Was Sojourner Truth.* Appleton-Century Crofts, 1962.